DATE DUE

BRODART, CO.   Cat. No. 23-221

PRAISES FOR NO-FAIL-HIRING

"For many businesses the difference between success and failure often boils down to one thing--making good hiring decisions. Although there are numerous books on the subject, No-Fail Hiring is clearly the one book that quickly gives the reader the essential walkway points for effective hiring and an action plan in an easy to follow format. With all of the pressure of running a business in the real world, this book is the real-world solution to achieving success in business by hiring and retaining the best."

Lester S. Rosen, Attorney at Law, author of "The Safe Hiring Manual",
President of Employment Screening Resources (ESR)
co-chair of NAPBS (National Association of
Professional Background Screeners)

"All I can say is WOW! The title in no way does this book justice! This is not a book, but a bible on hiring and retaining excellent staff. Honestly, I cannot wait to have all my key staff read this in its entirety! However, it is also an amazing reference tool. Any small business owner or HR professional should study this work and know it cold. There is nothing like this on book shelves that I have ever seen. I feel my eyes have been opened to host of processes that will save us thousands upon thousands of dollars. VERY well written! "

Joy Gendusa, CEO PostcardMania (Inc. 500).

"No-Fail Hiring is an absolute MUST read for anyone making hiring decisions! There are many books on this subject, but none as hard hitting and specific as what Patrick Valtin and L.D. Sledge have put together. From the "10 Deadliest Hiring Tips" at the beginning of the book to the "No Fail Hiring Tips" summary after each chapter, this book is an interesting and informative read that pulls no punches and gets right to the point. There is a PHD in hiring between the covers of this brilliant piece of work." -

Marsha Friedman, CEO EMSI Public Relations, author of
"Celebritize Yourself" and national talk radio show host.

"In today's business environment, this is a must-read for every business and practice owner-entrepreneur who is planning on expanding a business or professional practice. I will be recommending it to all my clients. It's packed with easy to read, understand and apply, all you need to know about the good, the bad and the ugly in hiring, written by experts who know."

Freddie Ulan, DC, CCN, Chairman, Ulan Nutritional Systems

"I am the CEO of an energy company with a staff of 150. Hiring is a day to day function and even with all the other activity I perform, I have to ensure we are addressing hiring from a legal perspective. Without good people my company would not enjoy the affluence we have. I have searched for a reference on hiring, and have found a jewel! No Fail Hiring is a must read. It helps the manager and HR keep in tune with the changing times and covers every possible element from legal to marketing to the hiring process itself. It is going to become a trusted source in the business world.

Patrick J. Clouden , Chief Executive Officer of Consumer Energy Solutions, Inc., one of the nation's top energy consulting firms.

"This is the best book I have seen on this subject! It really gives great perspective and fantastic, workable tools in this area, one we can all benefit from! Get it and use it!"

Craig Ferreira, Chairman & CEO Survival Strategies, Inc.

"No Fail Hiring is a sourcebook, a guide, a roadmap, and a reference to successful hiring. It is the best out there on the subject."

Ben Kugler, Chief Operating Officer of dreamGEAR, LLC

"As a small business owner, I thoroughly enjoyed and appreciated this book! Happy, productive, and loyal employees are the heartblood of any business, but weeding out the undesirable and finding pearls is a daunting process, particularly now when many hires really   only sign on temporarily. On top of that, the grim spectre of lawsuits haunts every HR and CEO.

Now, we finally have a reliable guide to every aspect of the hiring process, No Fail Hiring. Easy to read and put into practice. Buy it, read it, use it.

Sue Moore CEO Bright Sky Learning LLC

"These days, hiring new employees can be a nightmare if you don't know what you're doing and how to filter the best candidates. Gut instincts will only serve you so many times but you are bound to "miss" as many times as you "hit" which is costly and wasteful both monetarily and emotionally to the business owner. This book is straight to the point with simple information that arms the business owner with need to know information that makes all the difference in the world. Hiring is the core to growth in any company which means knowing best practices related to hiring is vital and it starts with reading this book.

Robert Cornish, CEO Richter10.2 Media Group

"It would be a grave error for any CEO or HR to miss having this book as a ready reference. It should be THE book for managers who have anything to do with hiring."

Don Pearson, Executive Vice President, Group Publisher
Government Technology Media, a division of e.Republic, Inc.

"Hope is a word that describes lack of certainty in one's ability to get the desired result. When hiring a new employee it is truly vital to minimize the hope by maximizing the certainty. NO FAIL HIRING provides the needed and wanted information, viewpoints and guidelines to help you increase the certainty that you are hiring the right person, for the right reasons, for the right job. As an employer you want to create a certain culture within your organization - be certain, NOT hopeful, that your choice of who you hire will help enhance the vision for the culture you want to create within your organization - NO FAIL HIRING should be read, with no fail, by those who are involved in your hiring process.

Bernard Percy, President THE FOUNDATIONS OF BRILLIANCE
(a career and educational consulting organization)

"Wow! This book is long overdue. If you don't know the 10 deadliest hiring mistakes and how to overcome them, you lose more than just money. I have 150 employees and over the past 12 years we have interviewed thousands of prospective employees. I had to learn "hiring" the hard way. I wish this book was written before I started my first business! Even though I have had to learn many lessons on my own, I still found several helpful solutions for specific hiring and retention problems.

Read this book from beginning to end and then apply it!"

Jim Mathers, President Consumer Energy Solutions, Inc.

"The thing I remembered most about her was her green eyes; they made me think of a rain forest. Pretty girl, not quite movie star gorgeous, but blond and fashion runway tall. I met her when I had gone to visit a friend who had a medical device company in Covina. She was the Controller. She was also a crook.

Months later, my friend told me he had discovered a discrepancy in the bank account. Turns out she had embezzled almost $300,000 from his company over a period of 5 years. Really hard to figure. She had a husband and a couple of kids. But it seems the husband liked to gamble, and...

If you don't read another thing this quarter, read Patrick's book. There is no greater mandate for a CEO than hiring the right people. This book tells you exactly how to do just that. Would have saved my friend a small fortune and a lot of grief. The information in this book is vital for CEOs and HR directors. It gives you the tools to build your company on a foundation of productive and supportive employees, and these days, it doesn't get better than that.

John Truman Wolfe, Best Selling Author of
Crisis by Design The Untold Story of the Global Financial Coup

"As owner of a construction business for the last 25 years, I have employed several thousand people; most of the time I did it the hard way. I wish I had read the book 'No-Fail Hiring' years ago. I have never seen such a great reference to understand the subject of hiring and retaining the best employees as is found in 'No Fail Hiring.' Every step is there and all the traps are revealed. This is a must-read for every smart business owner and anyone who does hiring."

Michael Chan, CEO The Durable Group

"There is no silver bullet in running a successful business: it is doing many little things, just right. I know, I own a business with 150 employees. Getting the right people controlling their areas of responsibilities is the key to anyone's success. This book has many gems of wisdom; it will help educate my managers on what to be thinking and looking for when they need to promote staff into key posts in their areas and how to protect our company from the litigious society we live in today. Thank you for taking the time to put these key points in an easy-to-read reference source. God knows the small businessman needs all the help he can get."

Tom Cummins, CEO CSS, LLC

"When you match real world experience with an ability to organize and a purpose to make positive things happen, you get a book that is insightful and practical. Patrick Valtin, in his book, No Fail Hiring, provides workable tools to ensure that any business owner achieves the growth he or she desires by having the vital element of predictable and effective staff/employee support."

Arte Maren, Author of
The Natural Laws of Management: The Admin Scale

"Maybe this book should be called the Encyclopedia of Hiring Error Avoidance. The breadth of the work is encyclopedic, with the authors having done all of the research, distillation, and collation of data we entrepreneurs could never have the time to do ourselves. Nor should we take the time! We have a business to found and expand! Let the guys at No Fail Hiring clear away those trip wires for us! But wait. There's more. They then also provide straightforward hiring principles I can build into any part of my business to keep me from running off the rails to success."

Thomas A. Wright, Managing Director, Emory Capital Management, LLC

"As an attorney who has learned the hard way about hiring the wrong people, I found "No Fail Hiring" to be a delightful and most informative read. There are many tips and explanations that will help anyone understand not only the right way to hire but also the way to avoid the increasing number of legal pitfalls. It is a very unique book that all business owners and people responsible for hiring should read and keep at their desk."

Steve Hayes, Attorney at Law

"Taking the hiring process for granted is risky business. I run the technical division of a large software firm, where the success of the entire company rides on our ability to hire and keep the best technical talent. Not only does this book teach you how to attract and select great employees, but it also shows how to KEEP great employees once you have them. In my business, the people ARE the competitive advantage – not something I want to leave to risk. This book is one of those rare gems that takes a complex topic and delivers it in simple terms that you can immediately apply."

Mark Patton, Vice President of Research and Development, GFI Software

"It is not often you find a book on better selection that is as pragmatic and practical as this one. It not only tells you what you need to do to hire better employees but gives you the tools, tips and technique you need in a simple to use and understand manner."

Mel Kleiman, CSP, Author of *Hire Tough, Manage Easy,* President of Humetrics, Inc.

NOFAIL HIRING

HIRING

**Your Ultimate Guide to Attracting
And Recruiting Top Players
In a Troubled Economy**

Your Ultimate Guide to Attracting And Recruiting Top Players In a Troubled Economy

Patrick V. Valtin
with L. D. Sledge, J.D.

Published by <u>M2-TEC PUBLISHERS, a branch of M2-TEC USA, INC.</u>

For general information on our hiring training/coaching services and any other services or for technical support, you can contact our customer service department at 877-831 2299. You can also send a fax to (727) 449 0979 or e-mail at info@m2-tec.com. Websites: www.nofailhiring.com or www.m2-tec.com

Library of Congress Cataloging-in-publication data:

Patrick V. Valtin, with Lawrence D. Sledge.
NO-FAIL HIRING: Your Ultimate Guide to Attracting and Recruiting Top Players in a Troubled Economy.

ISBN 978-0-9798586-7-3

Library of Congress Control Number (LCCN): 2011903729

1. Business/Management   2. Personnel selection 3. Human Resources   4. Employee Recruitment

arde.com

TABLE OF CONTENTS

ACKNOWLEDGEMENT

I would never have been able to write this book if I had not had the honor and privilege to serve thousands of clients across the world who attended my training or coaching sessions on the subject of hiring and who successfully applied the principles presented herein. I admire you so much for making things happen. Your daily work contributes to the wealth of your community and of your nation; I am infinitely thankful for your support, your feedback and your continuous help.

I want to thank all my international partners from West and Central Europe, Russia, Israel, Taiwan and the Americas who have been inviting me, year after year, to educate their clients on the subject of hiring, marketing, sales and business strategies. Specifically, my deepest admiration to my partners at U-Man Belgium, who for the last 22 years have relentlessly demonstrated their leadership in providing the highest quality of training to thousands of business owners and employees. Their dedication has always been and remains a primary source of motivation for me to work harder and smarter at helping others.

Joy Gendusa, CEO of PostcardMania, has been a source of inspiration since I started my activities in the USA. She is an amazing being who has a unique talent to make big things out of nothing. When she told me a few years ago to write a book, she probably had no idea of the consequences of her suggestion.

To Marsha Friedman, author of "Celebritize Yourself", whose book and market knowledge closed me on the idea that I, too, could write a successful book to share my passion for new ideas and knowledge.

To Lester S. Rosen, author of the excellent "Safe Hiring Manual" and president of "Employment Screening Resources (ESR), who, I believe, has written the best book ever on personnel selection. Mr. Rosen's professionalism has driven me to write my book as best as I could. Unknowingly, he has raised my personal standards to higher levels than I had ever expected, as an author.

To Marten Runow – founder of Performia International, who has been a wonderful source of inspiration and a friend for the last 23 years. Marten knows more about personnel selection than anyone else I have worked with in the last 24 years. If you ever look to hire a great motivational-inspirational speaker on the subject of People Management, I recommend him first.

To my close friends and business mentors who have faithfully supported me in this writing adventure: Pat Clouden, Jim Mathers, David Tourje, Don Pearson, Tom Wright, Steve Hayes, Freddie Ulan, Craig Ferreira, Ben Kugler, Sue Moore, Robert Cornish, Bernard Percy, Glenn Wahlquist, John Truman Wolfe, Michael Chan, Tom Cummins, Chuck and Marina Simons, Mark Patton, Ido Fischler, Bud Reichel, Roger Vanloocke, Tamas Mondovics, Giannis Bogdanos, and many more.

To Jim Criscoe, internet research specialist, who spent more hours than I could count on finding the best data for allowing us to assemble this book. Jim naturally did more than we expected and was definitely a key element in the development of our work.

To Karen Walby, for editing this book from the very beginning and for kindly leading the way to getting a real product out of it.

To all my partners in the ExecLife® Coaching Group who thrive on a daily basis to improve conditions for business owners and their employees. These people are the best and most dedicated professional trainers & coaches you can ever work with. When results count they show the way.

A very special gratitude to L.D. Sledge, who definitely is the best partner and co-author I could dream of for writing on the subject of hiring. A successful court attorney for 43 years in Louisiana, L.D experienced the dangers of a wrong hire "first hand," which led him to lose his practice. His personal commitment to help business owners avoid the legal and financial trouble he himself went through has been the driving force behind every page of this book. When you meet L.D. in one of our lectures or hear him on the radio, you will understand why you cannot resist loving him. L.D. has been my first angel throughout the writing of this book.

To Daniel and Darlene Swanson, our book & jacket designers, who have shown more patience and tolerance for our mistakes than we could hope for. Their expertise and care were the best bonus we could get and if you ever happen to write a book, contact them.

Finally for their continuous supportive encouragement and ongoing technical & administrative assistance, I thank the love of my life – my wife Chantal, together with my children Anne Caroline and Steve who provided me with the original research material that made the writing of this book possible. And to Nathan who never complained about the impossible hours I had to spend on getting this book off the press. Their patience and never-ending love were more than often the fuel that allowed me to keep going.

– Patrick Valtin

Introduction

"Over the next few years, recruiting will make a sharp departure from the recent past. With a looming talent shortage – complicated further by pent-up demand among employees to change jobs – the rise of the social Web as a communications platform, and the higher expectations of the Millennial generation, recruiting is entering a new, more challenging era."

Scott Melland,
Chairman, Dice Holdings, Inc.
"The Future of Recruiting" (1)

WHO WOULD THINK OF HIRING TODAY? _____

Dear Reader and Business Owner,

Our hat is off to you as an entrepreneur, risk taker and creator of wealth. It is on your back that the economy moves at all today. And it is upon your personal actions, not some "New Deal" political giveaway, that we have a chance for a brighter tomorrow.

You must be a maverick at heart to be willing to persevere in today's economy. As we go to press, U.S. unemployment is hitting the 10% mark. But the more real, yet unknown, unemployment rate, called *U6*, is nearing 18% and heading toward 20% by 2011. America is experiencing its worst economic crisis since the Great Depression. And crisis forces change.

So then, why publish a book on hiring NOW? To lend support and sound the warning of what is to come. On top of the "normal" frustrations and headaches associated with hiring, we are facing a changing social structure in America which portends tremendous dislocation in the job market. The war for talent is raging more than ever; government involvement and regulations are on the rise.

As the European employment model has shown for decades, the higher the unemployment rate, the more exasperating it is to find qualified, motivated and honest employees. Increasingly, we see a volatile, disloyal employment market, with other employers desperately competing for the best they can find.

Within this environment, you need a competitive edge, a *No-Fail Hiring* Guide to attract and recruit the top players, so you can surround yourself with honest, able and dedicated people who share your core business values, while appreciating your performance standards.

As hiring regulations from federal and state bureaucracies erode employers' rights in an off-target move to stimulate employment, you will also avoid a lot of legal trouble in your expansion-minded hiring efforts with this practical and down-to-earth *No-Fail Hiring* Guide.

It might even save your business.

NOFAIL
HIRING

Part A

Before You
Start

Spending more time attracting and selecting the right people will save you much more time by NOT having to manage them!

Chapter 1

Your Most Important Job

"One of the most important aspects of being a superior leader is hiring people smarter than you. Top leaders spend more time putting the right team in place to accomplish their objectives than they spend on planning, strategizing, or many other components of their job."

Bob Prosen, author of
"Kiss Theory Good Bye" [1]

THE 1,000% LEVERAGE FACTOR

You are growing your business through difficult times and you are planning on expanding even more, "no matter what." If you are like most business owners, your company survival has been relying mostly on your 14-hour workdays as well as on the shoulders of a few dedicated employees.

What is your most precious resource in the company? Where does the real treasure of your business truly lie? What is your most valuable asset? It is not buildings, fleets or patents. No, it is PEOPLE!

But wait a minute: where does 95% of all your daily trouble come from? Yep, you are right: it comes from people!

Hold on another second: what do 95% of business owners put most of their attention on, on a daily basis? You got it: making things go right so they can make money!

Make a list of all your current serious business challenges or problems, whether related to increasing sales, improving productivity, handling important clients, etc. You will find out that behind each of these, there is someone who did not do his/her job. Someone did not do what you expected him/her to do – and you probably ended up doing the work yourself!

You might need to develop stronger leadership skills. But guess what: good employees need good *relationships,* more than strong leadership. Bad employees do not respond to leadership, neither to relationships; they only respond to repetitive orders and threats.

Do you want your company to expand and make more money? Do you want to be able to focus on those activities that provide the best return for your business?

Well then, here is your most important job: hire people who will genuinely help your company expand and prosper, while leaving you to do what you really love to – and should do! Then, your business will grow with less pain, stress and frustration!

After directly working with over 75,000 business owners around the world in all kinds of industries in the last 24 years, we have concluded that over 55% of business failures and 84% of serious business crises are not due to unfavorable economic environments, lack of resources or lack of marketing power:

They are due to bad/wrong hiring decisions!

Hiring right definitely provides the most powerful leverage for your business. In fact, we call it the 1,000% leverage factor, or *the factor of 10* – for the following reasons:

✓ Hiring is a dangerous bet which can directly impact profitability. A new employee who is fired within three months can cost up to 10 times what you invested to get him/her on the job.

✓ If you fire a bad hire or lose a good one after one year, the consequent financial, organizational and emotional losses can add up to 10 times the yearly salary and other compensations.

✓ Hire the right person for any job and you will find out that his/her real value in the company can be multiplied by a factor of 10 compared to his/her cost of employment. Besides doing the job, that employee is sparing you headaches, worries and/or costly mistakes. He/she is also saving you valuable time – which allows you to concentrate on what you should be doing to expand the business!

Have you ever heard of any investment opportunity offering you a potential return of 1,000%? We haven't. But we know that investing in the right people not only provides the best return for your business, but also the luxury of reducing stress, worries and uncertainties about the future. And yes, it does start with recruiting and posting.

DID YOU KNOW?

Dunn and Bradstreet's research shows that 96% of businesses in America fail due to managerial incompetence. Specifically, per Jessie Hagen, former VP at U.S. Bank, 56% of business failures are due to hiring mistakes such as hiring friends, relatives or people without checking if they had the needed skills.[2]

KNOW IT BEFORE YOU DELEGATE IT

Over 85% of business owners recognize that hiring is too painful of an experience to try to become great at it. They would rather delegate the job to someone more "knowledgeable."

Add the current economic conditions and you discover that for most, hiring is an unworthy task in the daily management of their business. It is true that when fighting to survive, a company's main concern is to reduce the cost of doing business – and employees represent the largest area of expenses. Therefore hiring is often relegated to secondary, future plans.

Then, when you realize you can't hold down the fort all alone, working overtime every day of the week, the most common reaction is to "delegate" this strategically vital hiring function to experts or professionals who make a living out of it.

Don't take it badly. There are some extremely effective, experienced recruitment firms/headhunters out there who can do the job. But once you recognize the strategic importance of hiring right, it would seem suicidal to delegate this function without being able to control the quality of WHAT is being done.

Would you ever delegate a vital function without being able to control it? This would be a sign of gross managerial incompetence, wouldn't you agree? Look at some of the most successful entrepreneurs in American history and you will find out that they consider hiring the most strategically vital part of their work:

◆ *"If we weren't still hiring great people and pushing ahead at full speed, it would be easy to fall behind and become a mediocre company."* – **Bill Gates** [3]

◆ *"I hire people brighter than me and then I get out of their way."* – **Lee Iacocca** [4]

◆ *"Recruiting is hard. It's just finding the needles in the haystack. You can't know enough in a one-hour interview."* – **Steve Jobs** [5]

When it comes to delegating a task or function, especially hiring, you MUST respect the following golden rule:

Do not delegate something over which you have no or little control. Delegating without control is called "dumping" (like dumping a problem on someone else). This is a sure way of inviting trouble and inheriting the job back in a worse condition.

You are less likely of being "screwed" by your accountant if you are educated on the subject of accounting, right? Likewise, you are less likely to be disappointed by a bad hire if you are properly educated on the subject of people and hiring. Furthermore, this applies to all your partners, executives or anyone else involved with the hiring process.

As mentioned earlier, "hiring right" is the most neglected management function. As for the perceived importance of hiring, only 35% of female small business owners want to hire new employees to push expansion – compared to 66% of male small business owners.[5]

Have you ever really learned something useful and workable on the subject of the human mind – such as: *how do you measure loyalty, honesty or even ability to perform?* No, not really. Would it make sense to know something about it? Yes, absolutely! People: the most important and precious resource in the company…yet the most unknown one!

What about hiring an outside recruitment firm? Here is the catch: they can't always be fully blamed for hiring failures. Lack of proper understanding

DID YOU KNOW?

According to the U.S. Department of Labor, 50% of applicants stay only 6 months in their job. Also, over 60% of all employees stay less than 5 years.[7] It seems that you have equal chances of success in hiring as you have in just flipping a coin.

in the hiring process is the main enemy to successful hiring. Second is lack of clearly expressed expectations (by the employer). Next is lack of honesty in the formulation of these expectations. We could go on, but bluntly speaking, the business owner is always behind a hiring failure.

Being well prepared for your next hiring mission starts with the following state of mind:

a. Recognize that expanding your business at optimal speed and minimal cost (financial, organizational and emotional) is directly dependent upon hiring right. It is a strategic move that can affect your business more than any other decision.

b. Get personally educated on the subject of hiring. Reading this book is a great move toward greater effectiveness!

c. Educate your partners, executives and key employees on the importance of understanding and being involved in the hiring process. Minimally, have them all read this book.

d. If you work with a professional recruitment firm, do not just "dump" the responsibility on them. Ask to coordinate and be briefed on their working methods. You must be able to understand AND control the full hiring cycle.

e. Ideally, you want to develop a standard hiring procedure within the company. This book provides a good outline of what needs to be done to have a better control on the subject. We can also help you establish a full hiring department. Our specialty is to train you and any other concerned executive(s), so that hiring can be done with full understanding and control, no matter who you need to select and put on post.

DID YOU KNOW?

✓ In 2008, the average yearly employee theft case was $2,672. [8]

✓ 30% of all business failures are caused by employee theft. [9]

✓ The FBI calls employee theft the fastest growing crime in America. 55% of perpetrators of employee theft are managers. [10]

✓ FBI studies estimate that nearly 355,000 businesses will experience a workplace violence episode in any given year. [11]

✓ In 2008, the majority of retail shrinkage was due to employee theft at $15.9 billion, which represented almost half of losses. [12]

THE 10 DEADLIEST HIRING MISTAKES

Many books have been written on the subject, yet most of them are missing the boat when it comes to detecting the most fundamental and costliest mistakes business owners make in hiring new employees. In this book, we provide valuable tips to help you avoid the painful consequences of such deadly mistakes. Here is a glimpse:

Deadly mistake #1: No awareness of the legal aspects in hiring. Legal issues regarding hiring are often neglected by the employer. For example, if a dangerous, unqualified or dishonest employee is hired – and harm occurs – the employer faces the potential of a lawsuit for "negligent hiring" (see chapter 2). Worse yet, a bad-hiring decision can result in loss of business and damage to a professional reputation that may take years to correct. And if the business is sued, there is often little that can be done to show due diligence. Not knowing who you hire is like playing Russian roulette with the future of your business.

You must develop precise policies and procedures which monitor and guide the hiring process, in compliance with employment laws. These procedures must be clearly communicated to every candidate prior to the interview. One important policy to apply is related to the standardization of your pre-employment screenings and/or background checks: no candidate should be allowed to avoid such actions. By getting all of them through such procedures, you force those who have something to hide to either be honest or to look for another job. And you protect yourself legally!

Deadly mistake #2: The long-term strategy is unclear. The company hires simply because there is an empty spot to be filled. Top management is unaware that providing a clear picture of the company's future and related challenges, is a vital criterion to attract good candidates in your hiring messages.

If you don't seem to see the future, the applicants will not either. GOOD applicants want to have a clear vision of your company's plans. They also want to feel that there are opportunities and challenges awaiting them, so they can prove their ability to achieve things. "Knowing where you are going" is a priority to successful hiring.

Deadly mistake #3: The marketing approach is inappropriate. Most business owners develop a very conservative attitude when faced with hiring challenges. They do not understand that GOOD candidates have the power of selection in their job search. You are just one amid tens of thousands of other employers, looking for the best.

Good candidates know they have the power of choice. They are more selective and more demanding when faced with multiple job opportunities. Your attitude in hiring should be one of a marketing manager, faced with too many competitors going after your (few) potential customers: "what do I need to do, to attract good candidates, even before they show up at the hiring interview?"

Deadly mistake #4: The job opportunity is too good to be true. Too often, employers avoid being clear and honest in regards to the company's weak points or internal challenges. They do not want to discourage applicants. Later on, when these concealed challenges or difficulties appear, the new employee feels cheated... and leaves.

Apply the *law of transparency* throughout the procedure. Be as precise as possible in your expectations and don't be afraid to describe a realistic scene of the situation. Unqualified, scared applicants will run away. The good ones will love the challenges. Clearly describe what you expect from new employees in terms of results, daily actions and behavior; they will be less likely to rebel soon after being hired.

Deadly mistake #5: Gut-feelings lead the pre-selection process. A "pretty" resume does not necessarily reflect a qualified applicant. Lack of formalized, objective specifications in the pre-selection process can cost management time and energy in "blindly" analyzing each incoming resume. No one knows exactly what to look for.

Objective, measurable and easily recognizable specifications for pre-selection qualifications must be specified. All concerned in the hiring must then be informed of these specifications, in order to accurately measure the degree of qualification of an applicant.

These qualifying criteria must be based on experience and successful actions. The best way to specify an "ideal profile" for a future employee is to look for an existing successful profile within the company, especially regarding important "soft skills" (see next chapter).

Deadly mistake #6: Falling into the personality trap. Many of us remember being seduced by an applicant with a pleasant attitude who demonstrated good relational skills during the interview — but did not demonstrate acceptable performance, once on post. Most interview techniques are limited to measuring *momentary* personality rather than performance potential. A strong personality can generate dislike or suspicion. However, it can also reflect the candidate's strong desire to attain results. "Nice" people aren't always the most effective ones.

Your first priority is NOT to find out if an applicant has a nice personality but to answer the following question: "Will the applicant achieve the required results for a specific position?" In other words, what is his or her potential ability to reach specific results on the job, within a specific working environment? The personality-related evaluation criteria are most often subjective; they do not reflect the candidate's future attitude and performance. What you see today may very well be completely different tomorrow!

Deadly mistake #7: The applicant controls the interview. Eager to fill the job opening quickly and worried about losing a good candidate, the employer usually makes two fatal mistakes: (1) he/she talks too much and (2) he/she does not find out enough critical and measurable elements about the candidate's potential (a consequence of the first mistake). In a non-structured interview, the candidate who speaks the best commonly comes out winning the job.

Your questions must be structured and formalized in order to obtain visible and objective selection criteria, such as: the aptitude to get results and the lasting personality rather than the momentary one. A hiring interview must be controlled by the employer – not by the candidate. It is your job to make the candidate talk and reveal his/her true, lasting personality. But don't let him/her say just anything…you must obtain vital information that will enable you to detect his/her true potential to obtain results on the specific job.

Deadly mistake #8: Dangerous invisible factors are neglected. Undetected weaknesses are commonly the ones that lead to failure. Diagnostic supports are often used (such as personality, honesty or skill tests), in order to reinforce one's impressions. Unfortunately, their reliability is often questionable. One of the most serious problems is the confusion associated with a candidate's momentary and lasting personality. Using such tests as quality control tools does not assist the employer in determining the candidate's true performance potential.

You cannot hire someone solely based on what is observed during the interview. Within a few months, a costly disappointment can result from many "unseen" personality factors. Detecting elements of the candidate's "lasting" personality is vital if you want to adequately predict his/her behavior and productivity level. Make sure the test you use takes this "temporary" personality into consideration (most don't).

Deadly mistake #9: Subjectivity rules. Without precise and standard evaluation criteria, one can miss vital information or mis-evaluate its relative importance. Too often the final decision is based on personal opinions, rather than on objective evaluation criteria. Hope for success rather than probability of success is the norm. Each concerned manager is defending or justifying his/her viewpoint. What pleased one, displeased another, and no one is completely reassured. Lacking formalization, the hiring procedure remains a game of luck.

You must determine a list of evaluation standards, used by all managers involved to analyze an applicant's potential. Each must be able to measure the same criteria so as to prevent subjective factors from influencing the final hiring decision. Anyone involved in evaluating a candidate's potential must understand AND apply these standards. Only then can a final selection be made objectively.

Deadly mistake #10: Efforts are limited to the hiring process. The new employee seldom has a formalized line of conduct to follow in order to succeed on the job. It is commonly referred to as the "Tom-Tom" drums law: you explain what is expected once, and then let the new employee figure it out! *"That's how everybody learned here…"*

You must incorporate a formal plan in order to ensure a successful integration of the new employee. This plan must include a complete checklist with sequential actions that must be mastered in order to be quickly operational. The candidate must be aware of what will be done within the next 3, 6 and 12 months, in order to help him/her develop his/her skills and performance. A formal job integration and appraisal plan brings comfort and stability to a new employee who has much to learn before even thinking of performing.

DID YOU KNOW?

If you own a small business (defined by the Small Business Administration as employing less than 500 people), you are a key contributor to the national economy – much more so than all big corporations considered together. As a matter of fact, per the SBA, small firms: [13]

◆ Represent 99.7% of all employer firms.

◆ Employ just over half of all private sector employees.

◆ Pay 44% of total U.S. private payroll.

◆ Have generated 64% of net new jobs over the past 15 years.

◆ Create more than half of the nonfarm private gross domestic product (GDP).

◆ Hire 40% of high tech workers (such as scientists, engineers, and computer programmers).

◆ Made up 97.3% of all identified exporters and produced 30.2% of the known export value in fiscal year 2007.

◆ Produce 13 times more patents per employee than large firms; these patents are twice as likely as large firm patents to be among the one percent most cited.

Why are we bringing this up? Simply because we feel it's important to stress the fact that small businesses make up the real heart and core of our nation's economy.

The creativity and efforts that you pour into your business can be further rewarded if you become more aware of the following truth: every time you hire a good employee and you do your best to bring him/her up to a high level of productivity, you improve your country's economy. It is also true that hiring good employees has become a daring, *maverick* enterprise. This book will help you meet the challenge.

NO-FAIL HIRING TIPS

➲ If you are expansion-driven, your most important job is not just to make things go right but rather to lead your employees to make things go right. Put more attention on hiring creative problem-solvers and dedicated employees who will be happy to save you time (and money) so that you can concentrate more on what you should – and love to do.

➲ Remember the 1,000% leverage factor or the factor of 10: there is no other business or management function that can offer a higher return than a smart hire.

➲ Most successful entrepreneurs in America are committed to hiring top performers; these can be attracted to YOUR business, depending on your own willingness to allow them to develop and grow with you.

➲ Hiring starts in your head! If you don't have the right state of mind, you won't attract the real earth shakers. A mediocre vision of the future will only attract mediocre applicants. Only the good applicants are looking for challenges and visionary leaders. Make sure you have a future to offer, or else you will suffer a horrible scarcity of good, motivated applicants.

➲ Learn how to avoid the 10 deadliest hiring mistakes. This book provides you with the fundamentals to help you dramatically improve your control over this vital yet too often neglected management function.

➲ Develop a standard hiring procedure in the company. Share the vision of hiring as a strategic tool with all your partners and/or executives. If you want to quickly set up the most efficient hiring department in compliance with all applicable laws, check out our unique workshop, the *No-Fail Hiring System*™ at www.nofailhiring.com.

If you think hiring costs you money, wait until you lose your business on a "negligent hiring" case!

Chapter

2

Legal Tips and Traps

"Unless a firm engages in due diligence in hiring, it is a statistical certainty that the firm will eventually hire someone with a criminal record."

Lester L. Rosen, author of *"The Safe Hiring Manual"*, President of *Employment Screening Resources (ESR)* [1]

A TOUGH LEGAL ENVIRONMENT _____

Increasingly, business owners are being held accountable for the acts of their employees. Multi-million-dollar jury verdicts are common, sometimes causing businesses irreparable financial damages: the median award for all employment-related claims in 2009 skyrocketed to $326,640, a 50% increase over 2008.[2] Here are the main federal laws prohibiting job discrimination, applying if you have 15 employees or more (ADEA/ADA: 20+ employees and EPA: no minimum):

✓ The Equal Pay Act of 1963 (EPA) prohibits discrimination in payment of wages to women with men performing essentially the same work.

✓ The "mother" of all Federal laws affecting employers is Title VII of the Civil Rights Act of 1964, signed into law by President Lyndon B. Johnson. This law prohibits discrimination based on sex, race, color, national origin or religion.

✓ The Age Discrimination in Employment Act of 1967 (ADEA) protects individuals who are 40 years of age or older.

✓ The Americans with Disabilities Act of 1990 (ADA) prohibits employment discrimination against qualified individuals with disabilities in the private sector, and in state & local governments.

✓ The Civil Rights Act of 1991, which provides for monetary damages in cases of intentional employment discrimination.

✓ Title II of the Genetic Information Non-discrimination Act of 2008 (GINA) which prohibits employment discrimination based on genetic information about an applicant, employee or former employee.

These acts are enforced by the **Equal Employment Opportunity Commission (EEOC)**. The EEOC has broad authority to investigate discrimination complaints based on an individual's race, color, national origin, religion, sex, age, disability and retaliation for reporting and/or opposing a discriminatory practice.

Ignorance of these federal laws can greatly affect your business. According to Clint Robison, a partner at Hinshaw & Culbertson, employers lose negligent hiring cases 75% of the time. The average settlement of such claims is $1.6 million.[3] Some examples:

✓ A federal jury awarded $2.3 million to a Los Angeles police officer who said she was sexually harassed and gave birth to a stillborn child because of the stress.[4]

✓ A Raleigh, N.C. Superior Court judge had ordered the chief executive of the Smithfield's Chicken 'n Bar-B-Q chain to pay a settlement reached last year to end a former male employee's sexual harassment lawsuit. Following a two-week trial, a jury in October 2007 ordered the company to pay $1.15 million to plaintiff for firing him after he had rebuffed sexual advances. [5]

✓ In the case of *Gregory Fishman v. MTA,* a federal jury awarded more than $700,000 to a former Queens-Midtown Tunnel employee who said his bosses denied him a promotion and penalized him for taking sick days because he was Jewish. Fishman heard his managers call him a "Jew" in a derogatory manner. Fishman took an exam for a promotion and earned the third highest score. He was passed over for a promotion, while people who had scored much lower on the test received the promotion, according to the complaint.[6]

✓ A federal jury in Manhattan recently found that Novartis Pharmaceuticals, a U.S. division of Novartis AG, discriminated against female sales representatives and ordered the company to pay $3.4 million plus $250 million in punitive damages to the dozen women who filed the lawsuit. [7]

The list of horror stories goes on by the thousands. And besides federal laws, there may be state-specific laws applying. The importance of not only being legally educated but mostly well prepared is evidenced by the following facts and figures:

◆ *The general civil caseload increased by 125% within 2 years. In contrast the employment discrimination case filings recorded a 2,166% increase.*[8]

◆ *Annual monetary benefits for ADA cases handled by the EEOC increased within a 6-year period from $0.2 million to $49.1 million.*[9]

◆ *Even when an employer prevails on a summary judgment, he has spent an average of $50,000 in attorney's fees.*[10]

DID YOU KNOW?

The Equal Employment Opportunity Commission (EEOC), the Civil Service Commission (CSC), the Department of Labor (DOL) and the Department of Justice (DOJ) jointly adopted in 1978 the *"Uniform Guidelines on Employee Selection Procedures."*

These guidelines incorporate principles designed to assist employers in complying with the requirements of Federal law. They provide a framework for determining the proper selection procedures, including the proper use of tests. You can download a full description of these Guidelines at the EEOC's website, www.eeoc.gov/policy/doc.

NEGLIGENT HIRING

Negligent hiring is the failure to properly screen employees, resulting in hiring someone with a history of violence or crime – and who commits a violent or criminal act. It normally refers to an employer's obligation to not hire an applicant that they know or should have known was likely to engage in criminal conduct against subject employees and even third parties.

Negligent retention is retaining an employee after the employer becomes aware of the employee's unsuitability (due to a history of violent or criminal acts), thereby failing to act on that knowledge. Either way, the company can be sued if the employer did not do an adequate background check on the new hire, or doesn't act when the employee manifests the unsuitable characteristics and harms another.

Negligent hiring and retention is a deadly weapon in the arsenal of plaintiff lawyers seeking recovery for their clients. When a lawyer prepares a lawsuit, every possible gun in that arsenal is brought out, fully primed and loaded. In case one doesn't hit the target and do the most damage, maybe another one will. It is called alternative pleading and it is done all the time.

In cases when lawyers are trying to reach into the deep pockets of businesses and their insurers, this course of action is like manna falling from heaven, providing outrageous judgments in states which allow punitive damages. Some examples:

- ✓ A furniture company paid $2.5 million for negligent hiring and retention of a deliveryman who attacked a customer in her home.[11]

- ✓ An employee with a criminal record sexually assaulted a child; $1.75 million was awarded for negligent hiring and retention.[12]

- ✓ A nursing home was found liable for $235,000 for the negligent hiring of an unlicensed nurse with 56 prior criminal convictions, who assaulted an 80-year-old visitor.[13]

- ✓ A twelve million dollar settlement was awarded in negligent hiring, training and supervision suit. The suit alleged an armored truck company did not adequately investigate its employees' past work records and did not provide adequate driving training.[14]

- ✓ An employer settled a suit for $2.5 million, seeking to hold it liable for negligent hiring and entrustment of an intoxicated security guard. The guard had an on-duty traffic accident in a company car which killed him and another motorist.[15]

- ✓ A store customer detained by a security guard as a suspected shoplifter was injured while being restrained and was awarded $10 million in damages in a suit against the store. He was claiming negligent hiring and training of guard and excessive use of force.[16]

✓ A $5 million settlement was awarded to the family of a deceased female tenant, in a suit against an apartment complex owner and management. The suit claimed that the tenant was killed by the brother of the complex's assistant manager and that it was negligent hiring to hire an assistant manager without a criminal background check.[17]

✓ A vacuum cleaner manufacturer was found liable for $45,000 because one of its distributors hired a door-to-door salesperson with a criminal record, who then raped a female customer in her home.[18]

Over 78% of our business contacts or customers had originally NEVER heard of negligent hiring. Most small to medium-sized business owners who had heard about it genuinely believed that it could only affect big corporations. Yet per the American Data Bank: [19]

✓ 45% of all applicants either have a criminal record, a bad driving record, a workers' compensation claim or a bad credit history.

✓ 95% of all companies in the U.S. are victims of theft, and yet only 10% ever discover it.

✓ Estimates of fraud committed by employees cost U.S. companies approximately $20 billion annually. Workplace theft tops out at more than $120 billion annually.

✓ 30% of all business failures are caused by employee theft.

Plaintiff lawyers revel in any new development that enables large judgments meaning larger fees. They are paid on a contingency basis, receiving a percentage of the amount recovered – sometimes up to 50% of the gross recovery. The attorney fronts all clients' expenses (many times all medical, even paying for surgery and support of the client), while the case is being prepared, litigated and appealed. He or she has much riding on winning, and will take every opportunity to ensure a win and therefore return of costs.

Being sued can be avoided. The following discussion and later chapters provide proven tips to help you minimize the liabilities of being caught in a negligent hiring case. Lawyers discern no difference between big and small companies – it is the evidence of a negligent hiring case that attracts them, no matter the size of your company.

RECORD KEEPING CAN SAVE YOU

How do you keep from being sued for negligent hiring or for violation of any of the other myriad laws that hang over your head like the sword of Damocles? How do you win if you are sued or assure yourself of any measure of security? The best way is to be meticulous in record keeping from the beginning of the hiring cycle through to the end.

The EEOC and the Office of Federal Contract Compliance Programs (OFCCP) have rules that must be followed, and these include record keeping. A grim example of failure to comply with these requirements is the recent case of Goodyear Tire and Rubber Company being ordered by an administrative law judge to pay $925,000 in back wages to 800 female job applicants who alleged hiring discrimination at a Goodyear plant in Virginia. Goodyear also agreed to hire 60 of the women, conduct annual training for plant managers and provide semi-annual reports to document compliance. It was all because of a failure to maintain adequate records to prove compliance.[20]

What can you do to comply and protect your company? Precise record keeping is paramount because poor or missing records make it hard to defend yourself against lawsuits. You must be proactive. Record keeping begins early in the hiring process. Here are the essentials:

- ✓ **Job description** - Be sure it describes job functions precisely (in compliance with the ADA). It should also identify minimum and important qualifications that applicants need for a specific job.
- ✓ **Job posting** - Avoid limitations or exclusions on any physical basis. Make sure there is no discrimination in any form.

✓ **Job application** - Ensure it includes employment-at-will language, a statement of truth and an authorization to check records.

✓ **Interview notes** - Avoid writing any personal thoughts/comments on resumes. Document only valid (logical/observable) reasons for selecting or rejecting candidates. Make sure the interview procedure is standard for ALL applicants.

✓ **Offer letters** - Establish all the terms of, and clearly confirm the employment-at-will status of the relationship.

✓ **Reference & background checks** - Ensure you send out the FCRA (Fair Credit Reporting Act) notices and that you systematically document authorizations from each candidate/employee.

✓ **I-9 Verification** - We advise you make a copy of the documents offered as proof of the applicant's right to work in the U.S..

✓ **Agreements** - Ensure that you have a copy of signed statements in each employee's file concerning non-compete agreements, employee handbook receipts, employment-at-will agreements, etc.

✓ **Employee personnel file** – This file should always include a copy of awards, performance appraisals, time-off requests, discipline records, employee handbook receipts, training records, payroll authorization forms, benefits records, etc.

✓ **Medical records** – If needed and applicable, keep them in a separate, locked file with limited access. This file may also contain FMLA (Family and Medical Leave Act) records.

✓ **Workers' compensation** – Work-related injuries and all of the documentation which goes along with the injuries.

✓ **Time-off** - These records must be maintained.

✓ **Promotions** - Be sure to fully document the reasons for selecting the employee for the promotion. Why? It is not who was promoted who files the suit, but the one who feels he/she was passed over. Ensure you can defend your decision to promote one employee over another.

✓ **Discipline** - Progressive discipline records are particularly important because they are hard to challenge when you have a well-kept progressive discipline record.

DID YOU KNOW?

The following documents should *not* be a part of an employee's personnel record but must be maintained separately, for the purpose of respecting privacy:

✓ Benefits information

✓ Medical information or doctor's notes

✓ Authorization for deduction or withholding of pay

✓ I-9 form and supporting documentation

✓ W-4 form or other tax forms

✓ Internal or external investigations/claims of any kind

Not only is record keeping a vital tactic to protect yourself, it is also a legal obligation to keep specific employee records at all time. When hiring, you must know what information is necessary to keep on record regarding your employees, in order to abide by the laws. Most of these are federal laws (IRS, DOL, EEOC) and state laws (workers' compensation and unemployment).

Your company can be randomly selected by the Department of Labor for inspection to ensure that you are in full compliance with record keeping requirements. In such cases, you must have all employee files available within 72 hours.

Knowing how to stay in compliance with the DOL and IRS might avoid costly penalties. If you violate these record keeping requirements, you can receive a criminal penalty of up to $10,000 and/or imprisonment for up to 6 months (although usually a jail sentence can only be imposed for second and subsequent convictions).

Visit the Department of Labor's website for detailed information on record keeping. [21] From the time you hire a new employee and up to 4 years after employment termination, you must be able to provide the required information. Properly kept records can help you avoid big trouble.

EMPLOYMENT AT WILL

What does "at will employment" mean? It means you can keep your employees for however long you want. This also means you can fire them for any reason or for no reason at all, so long as it is not an unlawful or discriminatory reason – such as age, sex, race, national origin or disability. The "downside" is that it also means the employee can quit for any reason or no reason as well.

Lawful, nondiscriminatory reasons for terminating an at-will employee include:

✓ Merger with another company or business

✓ Workforce reduction

✓ Change in company direction and business focus

✓ Poor company performance

Employment-at-will is a tool that your employees can use to suddenly find new, "better" opportunities, without warning. In recent years, court rulings have made it more difficult for organizations to use an employment-at-will policy.

IMPORTANT: if your company wishes to use employment-at-will, it is necessary to state such policy both on the employment application and in the employee handbook. Failure to establish this policy in writing will potentially result in your company being at the mercy of courts.

Once a company makes a decision about which approach it is going to use with its employees, it must be careful to stick with that decision. Courts will find inconsistency in hiring policies suspect and prone to investigation.

To illustrate, Ed B. was hired by M&H Aluminum Sales as a sales representative. The employee handbook stated that the first 90 days on the job was a probationary period and that M&H had an Employment-at-Will policy.

An appraisal was completed on Ed's performance at the end of 90 days. He was evaluated favorably. Two months later M&H terminated Ed using the employment-at-will provisions of the employee handbook. Ed sued M&H for wrongful discharge and won.

Ed's lawyer argued that M&H's use of the probationary period coupled with the use of performance appraisals indicated that the firm terminated for cause only. The performance appraisal form did not contain an employment-at-will statement and the probationary period was shown to be an implied and accepted contract between employer and employee.

Final resolution of the case was an award of $740,000 to Ed. This award was based on the employee's projected lost wages, plus benefits from the date of termination through retirement age and for economic loss due to the breached implied contract.[22]

DID YOU KNOW?

Exceptions to the employment-at-will doctrine are classified into three general categories: (a) public policy, (b) implied contract and (c) good faith and fair dealing.

You can learn more about these exceptions in the *Monthly Labor Review* of January 2001 from the Bureau of Labor Statistics website. [23]

PRACTICAL TIPS:

✓ Ensure that your employment application forms as well as your employee handbooks, working rules, etc. cover specific "at-will" language. Avoid nebulous language that could lead an employee to believe he or she is covered by an oral, written or "implied" contract.

✓ Eliminate any promises of fair treatment, progressive discipline and permanent employment in any employee/employment document.

✓ Add a clause in your application forms & employee handbooks, such as the following:

"I understand that my employment and compensation are 'at will' and therefore can be terminated, with or without cause, at any time without prior notice, at the option of either the Company or myself. I further understand and agree that although other terms and conditions of my employment may change, this at-will-employment relationship will remain in effect throughout my employment with the Company unless it is specifically modified by an express written employment agreement signed by the Company and by me."

✓ Avoid, during the interview and at any other time, suggestions such as *"you could have a great future here"* or *"as long as you do well, you have a job,"* etc. These suggestions can be seen as an implied contract. An employee with an implied contract may not be terminated without just cause (meaning: a fair and honest cause or reason, acted on in good faith by the employer).

✓ Also avoid promises of promotion or pay raise after some time or offering a career.

✓ Avoid the term "probationary period." To the employee, it could have an implication of permanence. If you really want to use one, use clear language such as: *"An introductory period is a training period, the completion of which does not guarantee continued employment. Following completion of such probationary period, you still may resign at any time, without cause; the company still has the right to terminate your employment at any time, with or without cause."*

✓ Do regular performance evaluations. Standardize your termination method and do not deviate from it. Upon termination of an employee, have the employee sign a simple form that gives the date of termination. Do not specify in writing why the employee is terminated, as it is an "at-will" employment agreement.

Final considerations: always make sure you have your "at-will" employment agreement form reviewed by your lawyer, as state regulations may vary. Times are changing and in the last few years, small businesses have been a prime target of potential wrongful discharge lawsuits, filed by educated or well-advised employees or applicants. The employment-at-will agreement is still your best bet in terms of legal protection, but you need to be "smart" in your intentions.

LAWS ON TESTING

An estimated 8,000 organizations systematically perform personality or integrity tests as part of their hiring process. Almost 3,000 firms offer various assessments for hiring purposes. Although the use of personality tests in the employment setting has increased substantially in the past five years, neither their legality nor their effectiveness as a screening device has been established or disproved.

Are personality tests legal? Some states, such as Massachusetts, Minnesota, Rhode Island and Wisconsin, severely restrict or outlaw various personality tests. Massachusetts, for example, prohibits employers from requiring an applicant to take a written examination to determine honesty. So before you screen applicants, check with your attorney regarding what restrictions might apply in your state.

In states where these tests are legal, the challenges that you will most likely face are covered under Employment Discrimination and Invasion of Privacy Laws.

Disparate Treatment. An employment discrimination challenge to a personality test could take the form of a straightforward "disparate treatment" action, asserting discriminatory refusal to hire based on race, color, national origin, sex, religion, disability, age, marital status, sexual preference or orientation, or any other factor outlawed by federal, state or local law. Many personality tests look into these factors or related issues.

Employers may be influenced by such information and thereby hide their motives for refusing to hire. For example, questions on past drug and alcohol use raise disability discrimination issues. The tests that inquire into religious beliefs may lead to a religious discrimination lawsuit.

Title VII of the Civil Rights Act of 1964 contains a specific provision regarding testing. The title of this provision is "Employment Tests and Selection Procedures," and here is a guideline sentence taken from that section: *With respect to tests in particular, Title VII permits employment tests as long as they are not "designed, intended or used to discriminate because of race, color, religion, sex or national origin."* [24]

EEOC position. In the wake of recent years' proliferation of multi-million dollar judgments and settlements, the EEOC held a public meeting in May 2007 on Employment Testing and Screening. This led to the release of a fact sheet to assist employers in understanding how to avoid employment discrimination claims based on tests and other selection procedures. EEOC's main points of advice are: [28]

✓ "Employers should administer interviews, tests and other selection procedures without regard to race, color, national origin, sex, religion, age (40 or older), or disability.

✓ "Employers should ensure that employment tests and other selection procedures are properly validated for the positions and purposes for which they are used. The test or selection procedure must be job-related and its results appropriate for the employer's purpose. While a test vendor's documentation supporting the validity of a test may be helpful, the employer is still responsible for ensuring that its tests are valid under the *United Guidelines on Employee Selection Procedures.*

DID YOU KNOW?

Screening applicants with any test may cost you a lot of trouble and money if you violate the EEOC rules on testing. Examples:

◆ In 2006, the Eighth Circuit Court of Appeal affirmed a $3 million judgment in the EEOC v. Dial Corp. case. The company had used a strength test that would have excluded women from entry-level jobs. [25]

◆ In 2007, Ford Motor Company, two of its affiliates and the UAW settled a discrimination case for $1.6 million, stemming from a cognitive apprenticeship test that appeared to have excluded African-Americans. [26]

◆ Recently, the U.S. Department of Labor settled a hiring discrimination case with The Wackenhut Corp. in Aurora, Colorado. Wackenhut will pay $290,000 to each of 446 African-American applicants who had been systematically rejected by a screening procedure. [27]

✓ "If a selection procedure screens out a protected group, the employer should determine whether there is an equally effective alternative selection procedure that has less adverse impact and, if so, adopt the alternative procedure. For example, if the selection procedure is a test, the employer should determine whether another test would predict job performance but not disproportionately exclude the protected group.

✓ "To ensure that a test or selection procedure remains predictive of success in a job, employers should keep abreast of changes in job requirements and should update the test specifications or selection procedures accordingly.

✓ "Employers should ensure that tests and selection procedures are not adopted casually by managers who know little about these processes. A test or selection procedure can be an effective management tool, but no test or selection procedure should be implemented without an understanding of its effectiveness and limitations for the organization, its appropriateness for a specific job and whether it can be appropriately administered and scored."

The EEOC provides a uniform set of principles governing the use of employee selection and testing procedures. Per this document, the main liability attached to testing and other pre-screening and hiring procedures is "Adverse Impact."

Adverse Impact is defined as: "A substantially different rate of selection in hiring, promotion or other employment decisions which works to the disadvantage of members of a race, sex or ethnic group." [29]

For more information on testing procedures as part of your selection and hiring strategy, see chapter 9, *"Prelude to the Second Interview."*

ANALYSIS OF A HIRING HORROR STORY ⎯⎯⎯⎯⎯⎯⎯⎯

A physical therapist loses her highly successful practice soon after she hired an over-emotional assistant who was hiding her addiction to psychiatric and recreational drugs.

Jill owned and operated a physical therapy clinic in Texas. She needed a trained assistant therapist; she hired Jane so that all patients could be properly taken care of. Jane seemed to be personable and cheerful. Her resume reflected her degrees and experience.

What happened? Jane soon revealed a very nervous, unstable and fearful disposition. On one occasion, she was having more difficulties than usual with her boyfriend and became hysterical in front of the patients. Jill had to restrain her by grasping her by her upper arms to ensure that she would not hurt anyone in the practice.

Consequences. Jane filed charges of assault and battery. Jill was charged.

She had to pay a heavy fine and served several months on supervised probation. This ruined her reputation, causing her to close her office and relocate to another state to start all over.

What did Jill do wrong? Jill hired Jane on initial impressions rather than digging into her background and personality. Had she checked her background, she would have discovered that Jane had a psychiatric history and had been institutionalized. She was on psychiatric drugs during her employment and also did recreational drugs.

What should Jill have done? Jill hired Jane "on an impulse." She should have developed a job description for the position. She should have required Jane to demonstrate evidence of any specific qualification. She just trusted what she was seeing and fell into the temporary personality trap. She should also have requested a background check which would have warned Jane had been institutionalized.

Jill could have administered a good personality test which would have revealed hidden job-related personality traits and weaknesses. A good legal drug screening would also have revealed that Jane was addicted to psychiatric and recreational drugs.

NO-FAIL HIRING TIPS

➲ Get educated on the basics of legal procedures related to selecting and hiring personnel. They are all covered by the Equal Employment Opportunity Commission (EEOC). You can download the Guidelines at the EEOC's website.

➲ Negligent hiring can easily cost you thousands of dollars and potentially ruin your business. If you apply the principles presented in this book, you will know what to do to avoid such trouble.

➲ Make sure you develop a legally acceptable record keeping policy for all hires and employees. Keep these records for a minimum of 4 years AFTER employment termination.

➲ Have your employment-at-will agreement form reviewed by your lawyer, to make sure it does not contain any suggestion of written, oral or even implied contract. Do not communicate anything (verbally or in writing) that could lead an applicant to believe he/she was offered a contract.

➲ Before you implement any application form, agreement form or employee handbook, make sure you have them reviewed by your lawyer. They are not experts in the hiring process but they can help you save a lot of money by making sure you abide by the law.

➲ If you use any screening test, the best way to stay legally protected is to be able to demonstrate that it is entirely job-based and that it does NOT create an adverse impact.

➲ If you need help in implementing a hiring procedure that will minimize the risks of negligent hiring, visit www.nofailhiring.com to discover our special *No-Fail-Hiring System*™. This unique, practical program contains all the necessary steps to help you avoid these costly mistakes… and consequences. We can also help you implement a complete "no-negligent-hiring" procedure, with the help of your legal advisor.

Hiring top players should be a business owner's constant strategic commitment, rather than just a sporadic concern!

Chapter

3

It is All About Marketing

"The good-to-great leaders began the transformation by first getting the right people on the bus (and the wrong people off the bus) and then figured out where to drive it."

Jim Collins, author of *"Good to Great"* [1]

A TOUGH JOB MARKET GETS TOUGHER _____

Economic forecasts will always determine business owners' willingness and readiness to hire more employees. Nevertheless, no matter how gloomy or pessimistic these forecasts may be, they should not prevent you from looking to expand. Some of today's most popular U.S. giants were born in the middle of a devastating economic crisis: [2]

- **Procter & Gamble:** born in the middle of the 1837 financial panic.

- **IBM:** founded during the long-term Depression (1873 – 1896).

- **GE:** founded at the start of the 1873 financial panic.

- **United Technology Corp (UTX):** started with the Great Depression.

- **FedEx:** founded at the start of the first oil crisis of 1973.

In an interview by Jennifer Reingold of CNN Money, Jim Collins (author of *"Good to Great"*) expressed best how some of these great companies turned crisis into opportunity:

> *"These companies, when they went through the Depression, really understood that it was the caliber of their people that would get them through. If there's a storm on the mountain, more important than the plan are the people you have with you. The right people don't need to be managed. The moment you feel the need to tightly manage someone, you've made a hiring mistake."* [3]

With the right people, whatever comes up may be challenging but will always result in a positive situation. Here are some indicators of what might be crossing your way to expansion and to finding top players:

Too many lost jobs – Per Robert Reich (former Labor Secretary and now professor of Public Policy at Berkeley), since December 2007, the U.S. economy has shed 8.4 million jobs and failed to create another 2.7 million required by an ever-larger pool of job-seekers. That leaves us more than 11 million jobs short. The number is worse if you include part-timers who'd rather be employed full time, those working full-time at fewer hours, and those overqualified who keep their lower quality job. This means that we could be looking at five to eight years before catching up to where we were before the recession began. As Reich states, *"More Americans will be working, but for inadequate pay."* [4]

Too many long-term unemployed – Per Sara Murray of the Wall Street Journal, nearly half of the unemployed (45.9%) have been out of work longer than six months. Overall, seven million Americans have been looking for work for 27 weeks or more; but more importantly, most of them (4.7 million) have been out of work for a year or more. [5]

According to the PEW Economic Policy Group, this is the highest long-term unemployment rate since World War II. In contrast, during the severe recession of the early 1980s, the percentage of workers unemployed for six months or longer peaked at 23% in 1983. [6]

A gloomy picture for future employment – You may have heard of recent declining unemployment rates – falling under the 10% in early July 2010. But many employment experts recognize that the unemployment rate fell mainly because the labor force fell faster than employment.

The broader, yet quite unknown unemployment rate, *"U6"* (which includes discouraged workers, people working part-time involuntarily and underemployed workers) peaked at 17% in May 2010. [7] The previous peak was in 1994 when *U6* reached 12%. It came down to below 8% in 2001 and started to drastically move up in 2009. [8] We believe it might rise above 20% in the coming year.

Government-related employment will not help and is in fact likely to suffer more in the coming year, as many states face huge drops in tax revenues from the current sluggish economy. By June 2010, state and local governments shed some 242,000 workers since the peak in state and local government employment in August 2008, including 95,000 jobs in the first 6 months of 2010. [9]

DID YOU KNOW?

Per the Bureau of Labor Statistics (BLS), the professional and business services sector and the health care & social assistance sectors are projected to grow at more than twice the annual average of 1.0 percent for all industries, adding the most employment, 4.2 million and 4.0 million, respectively between 2008 and 2018. [10]

PREDICTING THE FUTURE

How is a tougher job market going to impact your search for productive, loyal and dedicated staff? More importantly, how is it going to affect your business expansion and profitability?

Prediction no. 1: The Federal Government will soon make hiring much more challenging – under the cover of offering huge incentives to companies for hiring the long-term unemployed. Expect new regulations which will make it much harder for you to dehire.

As the Federal and State Governments fail to contribute to the improvement of the job market, one easier way will indeed be to regulate it with drastic measures. The strategy is simple: start by making hiring easier (through measures such as tax credits or even bonuses for hiring) and then make it virtually impossible to fire those you have hired. We are also going to see more pressure from employment legislation to make employment-at-will safer for employees and more hazardous for employers. Add the ever-increasing war for talent and you can see why employment-at-will is going to favor employees more than employers.

Prediction no. 2: Too many applicants will be competing for those scarce positions. But do not fall into the trap of thinking this pool of abundance is good news for you. Many applicants will over-rate their skills and personality in order to get the job, creating a serious challenge for you to properly select the best. Remember: a single bad hire can cost between $60,000 and $120,000, depending on the job you need to fill.

The continuing economic struggle will lead more people to put their attention on money as the main motivator to get a new job. This is the worst thing that can happen to you as a leader. Money never buys real loyalty, but too often less honesty (see why in next chapter).

Employees' general attitude towards loyalty will indeed become a more alarming factor, as Joe Light suggested in a May 2010 Wall Street Journal article:[11]

✓ 60% of surveyed employees in a recent poll intend to leave their current job when the market conditions get better.

✓ Dice.com, a job board for tech professionals, asked members what could persuade them to stay in their jobs if they found another opportunity. More than 57% of the 1,273 surveyed said nothing could persuade them to stay. Of those who said they could be persuaded, 42% said they wanted a higher salary and 11% wanted a promotion.

Prediction no. 3: Honesty is going to be more than ever *the* major issue in pre-selecting applicants. The fact that dishonest employees can cost your company thousands or even millions of dollars is probably not news to you. But we believe this issue is going to become a much more serious concern. Besides observing a decreasing level of morale in the society, evidence of dishonest applicants lying in their searches for the perfect job is quite alarming:

✓ Per the Society for Human Resources Management (SHRM), 53% of job applications contain inaccurate information. [12]

✓ In a survey conducted by CareerBuilder.com, 49% of the 3,100 hiring managers surveyed had caught a job applicant fabricating some part of his/her resume.[13]

✓ 9% of job applicants falsely claimed they had a college degree, listed false employers, or identified jobs that didn't exist.[14]

✓ 34% of application forms contain outright lies about experience, education, and ability to perform on the job.[15]

✓ A 2003 study of 2.6 million job applicants showed that 44% lied about prior work experience, 41% lied about their education, and 23% of applicants falsified their credentials or made false claims on their resumes.[16]

This disturbing decline in ethics touches everyone from recent graduates to executives and can have serious implications for your organization. For that reason, pre-employment screening such as reference checks, background checks and criminal record checks should be an essential part of your hiring process (see chapter 11). Also, those lying on their resumes should be considered as high risks for fraud. Your hiring policy and documents should definitely include a clause of exclusion in the event significant misrepresentation on a resume is detected.

DID YOU KNOW?

Per the Association of Certified Fraud Examiners: [17]

✓ Occupational fraud and abuse costs organizations about $600 billion annually, or roughly 6% of gross revenue.

✓ The median loss caused by occupational fraud cases in the study was $160,000. Nearly one-quarter of the frauds involved losses of at least $1 million.

✓ Occupational fraud situations last, on average, 18 months before they are being detected.

Prediction no. 4: The real upcoming shortage is going to be more about quality, rather than quantity. Expect a tougher war for talent where skilled applicants feel almighty and experienced employees can leverage their real value for higher compensations with your competitors.

According to a recent survey by the global strategic research and consulting firm *Benenson Strategy Group:* [18]

✓ Nearly two-thirds of employers have difficulty in finding qualified applicants to fill vacancies.

✓ More than half of employers (51%) indicated that at least 16% of their workforces have a skill gap that affects productivity.

✓ The biggest frustration with employees' performance is about soft skills: severe deficits in such areas as work ethic, self-motivation, personal accountability, punctuality, honesty, communication skills, time management and professionalism.

Hiring right is going to be only one vital part of your business strategy. Retention is going to be the other key word, as many of your competitors will be making irresistible offers to your top players.

DID YOU KNOW?

In a 2009 report, 779 industrial companies were asked to predict availability of qualified workers over the next 2 to 3 years: [19]

✓ 38% of all respondents plan on increased shortages ahead.

✓ 38% of the most profitable companies see a moderate to serious shortage today vs. 25% of the least profitable companies.

✓ In the Midwest, 25% see moderate shortages and only 1% report serious shortages, whereas, in the Southwest, 45% report moderate shortages and 5% serious shortages.

Many companies consider technical skills as the most important ones in their hiring decisions. We do not adhere to such a position. In her great book *"The Hard Truth about Soft Skills,"* Peggy Klaus stresses the vital importance of soft skills in selecting your new hires: [20]

✓ Companies that effectively recognized personal excellence had triple the profitability—as measured by return on equity (ROE)—in comparison with firms that didn't.

✓ Three-quarters of surveyed employers said incoming high school graduates were deficient in soft skills. Additionally, 40% of employers said that the high school graduates they hire lack adequate soft skills competency for even entry-level jobs.

✓ 93% of the HR managers surveyed said technical skills are easier to teach than soft skills. The most in-demand soft skills are organizational skills (87%), verbal communication (81%), teamwork and collaboration (78%), problem solving (60%), tact and diplomacy (59%), business writing (48%), and analytical skills (45%).

✓ In a Job Outlook 2008 survey conducted by the National Association of Colleges & Employers (NACE), the top characteristics looked for in new hires by 276 employers (mostly from the service sector) were all soft skills.

The REAL shortage is going to be a lack of soft-skilled people of all ages. It is more challenging to develop soft skills than technical ones. Have you ever tried to improve an employee's willingness and commitment (without having to use the money bait), no matter how competent he/she was? Then you know what we are talking about!

THE OPPORTUNITY

In the face of this "not-so-optimistic" view of the future in the job market, what is your real challenge going to be? Mainly, you will need to work smarter at ATTRACTING qualified players – not just finding them! The good news is that we believe the current radical changes in the job market will be playing to the advantage of <u>smart</u> employers.

The employment market used to be more active among already employed people, with over 85% of openings filled by people already employed. We believe this will dramatically change in the coming years.

Current employees who are secretly looking for another job are now competing with many available applicants who may have the same or higher qualifications. Many of those who lost their jobs for reasons independent from personal performance may be more flexible on the pay side; they may also present better soft skills such as: better work ethics, willingness to work hard and to learn, etc.

Surprisingly, some employers have developed a negative attitude toward hiring people who have been unemployed for "too long" – falsely considering that looking for a job for more than 3 months is a serious indicator of lack of qualifications. Employment experts believe that companies are increasingly interested only in applicants who already have a job. Rich Thompson, Vice President of Learning and Performance for Adecco Group North America, the world's largest staffing firm, says that in 3 out of the last 4 conversations he's had about openings, this requirement was brought up.[21]

In his article *"Out-of-work job applicants told unemployed need not apply,"* Chris Isidore reports for CNNMoney.com that more job postings include restrictions such as "unemployed candidates will not be considered" or "must be currently employed." In that same article, Lisa Chenofsky Singer, a human resources consultant from Millburn, NJ, states: *"Most executive recruiters won't look at a candidate unless they have a job, even if they don't like to admit to it."* [21]

There is no law directly prohibiting discrimination against the unemployed, though advocates said the practice could be illegal if it had a "disparate impact" on minority groups. But in the current economic scene, 5.5 people are looking for work per each available position. Ignoring this vast pool of unemployed – many of them highly qualified AND willing to take on new challenges — is just plain unprofessional.

The best strategic mindset for business owners is to attract and detect qualified players who are willing to work rather than "enjoy" their unemployment benefits and who are ready to take on new challenges – sometimes at a starting lower pay. People who need a job have a level of necessity (to survive economically and socially) which can be judiciously used to pump up the energy and drive in your business.

You can and should take advantage of the upcoming competition between those unemployed solely due to the economic downturn and those who have a job. Do not assume that the latter are more qualified. What is certain is that they are more expensive.

In the current employment scene, a redefinition of the qualified, top player or applicant is needed, in order to know exactly who you want to attract in your next hiring mission.

Our definition of "top player" is:

An applicant who possesses, beyond basic technical skills, most of the soft skills needed to operate on the specific job and in your working environment. Some of the most vital soft skills in this crisis-driven economy are hard to detect: one must be challenge and result-driven, honest, accountable, able, willing to learn and improve, group-spirited, loyal and naturally persistent through difficulties.

The next chapters are dedicated to help you detect, attract AND select those "soft-skilled" applicants – taking full advantage of the opportunities presented by a much more competitive employment market. The war for talent is definitely raging but the war between rivaling applicants will help you negotiate better conditions with those who excel best on the soft skills side.

IT IS NOT (JUST) ABOUT MONEY

What motivates people to work? What incentives should you offer to attract AND keep top performing and dedicated employees? Is it all about paying them more than the competition would?

There is, of course, nothing wrong with paying a high performing employee a competitive salary. There is, however, everything wrong with considering that money is the only motivation in choosing a job. Per the *Public Agenda Foundation,* employees consider the following factors as the most important ones in keeping a job (in descending order): [22]

1. Being treated with respect on the job.
2. Interesting work.
3. Recognition for good work.
4. A chance to develop skills.
5. Working for people who are open to new ideas.
6. Ability to think for oneself rather than just carry out instructions.
7. Seeing the end results of one's work.
8. Working for efficient managers.
9. A job that is not too easy.
10. Feeling well-informed about what is going on.
11. Job security.
12. High pay.
13. Good benefits.

One nuance to the above: employees' perceptions of important job satisfaction factors does not necessarily reflect the real drivers of commitment and retention. What is needed is a better evaluation of where "money" stands on the scale with other criteria. What is it that could drive employees to naturally want to work hard for you – and be loyal to you? As studies show, what employees say and what actually drives them is quite different.

In an in-depth analysis of 4,500 workers and managers, the *Center for Effective Organizations (CEO)* reveals that what employees say is important to take a job is, in many cases, is very different from what actually drives retention and commitment (in descending order): [23]

What they say is important:
- Work/life balance
- Job security

- Financial rewards
- Influence/autonomy
- Professional satisfaction

Actual drivers of retention:
- Pay-for-organizational performance (group bonuses, profit sharing, etc.)
- Satisfaction with career advancement
- Innovation and risk

Actual drivers of commitment:
- Pay-for-organizational performance
- Innovation and risk
- Strategic clarity
- Influence/autonomy
- Adequate development opportunities
- Opportunity for career self-management
- Professional satisfaction

So what does this tell us? <u>One</u>: any relatively smart and prepared applicant will avoid telling you they are mainly money-motivated. You are going to have to find out because over 70% of them can't be trusted to openly discuss it.

<u>Two</u>: the top players (per our definition) will indeed include financial rewards in their decisions to join your company BUT will start by *judging* your company through other, more important factors (see next page for details).

<u>Three</u>: the major difference between these qualified players and the money-motivated ones will be found in their reaction to your open insistence regarding individual AND organizational performance!

What *really* motivates them? You can always evaluate an applicant against four general levels of motivation in finding a job, whether they are employed or available in the job market:

A. **Nature of the job.** Top players look at doing what they like to do. No matter how tough the job market conditions might be, you want to detect those who would not compromise their life-long aspirations too much. Changing one's professional direction on a regular basis reflects a lack of stability in one's intentions. Always give priority to those applicants who demonstrate persistence in their professional orientation. This is quite easy to detect through a resume or job application analysis.

With young applicants, it is important to detect why they decided to take a specific academic orientation. Were they purpose-driven or merely going through school without any specific future intention? Watch out for the purposeless applicants who mostly look for a job "to make a living."

B. **Salary and other compensations**. Qualified applicants know how much they are worth. Even if the current job market is a "buyer's market," make sure you offer your selected players an attractive package that will motivate them to work for long term rewards. You might be in a strong position in negotiating the terms at the start, but don't make the mistake of giving those qualified players an "excuse" to look at other opportunities, once the market reverts.

No matter the job, always offer performance-based rewards, such as bonuses or profit sharing. Young employees are naturally favorable to individual performance monitoring factors. But organizational performance factors should also be a part of your reward system. Reduce the fixed part of the salary and provide larger performance-based rewards which drive organizational efficiency as well as a commitment to the future.

Watch out for the skilled or experienced applicants who try to sell you their talent at a higher fixed salary with no desire for performance-related rewards. The coming years will be bright for you and your business, provided you are able to surround yourself with able, performance-oriented and group-dedicated, as well as future-driven collaborators!

C. **Working environment.** While your employees will say that they want a new job for better pay, the reality might be different. In a study of 700 employees, Professor Hochwarter at the University of South Florida reveals that people do not leave their company, they leave their boss. Nearly two out of five employees feel that their superiors frequently fail to honor their promises, and 37% say they do not give credit when due. Another 23% said their supervisors blame others to cover up mistakes or minimize embarrassment. Survey respondents indicated that they would be more likely to leave a job due to a difficult relationship with a supervisor than they would if they were just dissatisfied with their salary.[24]

Be aware that qualified applicants will first judge your company through the same irrational criteria as any potential customer would with a supplier. The recruiter's attitude, employees' friendliness, the smile on the receptionist's face, etc. are all factors which will attract – or scare away good applicants more than any other!

D. **Development/advancement factors.** Many applicants primarily search for job security. Top players do not care about it as much. They mostly want to be challenged and meet their potential. They are future-oriented and they want to prove that "they can do it." They instantly respond to those "mission impossible" types of assignments. To them, being part of a future-oriented team is a major reward by itself; financial reward comes as a bonus.

The key factor is: does the applicant want to take an active role in the expansion of your business? Is he/she responding positively to your challenges? Many employers tend to be too nice and too promising during the hiring process. The truth is: scare your applicants by being clear and totally transparent about the current challenges or difficulties. Then show them the future.

Top players will love it and might take up the challenge right there. Other applicants will naturally shy away from you, which is exactly what you want! If you don't offer challenges first, you will indeed attract the wrong prospects for the job. Job security should be the reward of creating and contributing to a bright future, not a God-given right that you, the employer, must assume for every challenge-shy employee. Challenge is THE keyword!

NO-FAIL HIRING TIPS

- ➲ Don't count on the near future to make it easier for you as an employer. The number of long-term unemployed and people who unwillingly left the job market will increase, no matter what authorities say. This will lead to more government-sponsored measures with the purpose of artificially energizing the job market. Do not fall for incentives to hire without doing your due diligence.

- ➲ Put your attention on attracting and selecting top players, per our definition. Do not negotiate cheap financial terms because the numbers of applicants is impressive. Some top players might compromise on pay in order to get the job now but will also be the first ones to be solicited by your competitors when market conditions change.

- ➲ The growing affluence of available applicants will make your hiring decisions much more difficult, as many of them will tend to embellish their skills and qualifications. You need to learn to detect important personality characteristics such as loyalty, accountability and other vital soft skills, as these will increasingly be the ones most difficult to find.

- ➲ Your hiring procedure must include an accurate technique to detect honesty. Pre-employment screening tools should be systematically used. The best time to evaluate an applicant's real intentions is the hiring interview. We provide a unique, confidential interview technique which detects 20 important soft skills, starting with honesty. Check our *No-Fail Hiring* workshop at www.nofailhiring.com.

- ➲ You should evaluate every applicant against the four general levels of motivation in finding a job. Do not fall in the trap of thinking that money comes first. In fact, never hire a candidate who is mostly money-oriented; he/she will leave you soon for the same reason he/she selected you.

For too many employers, hiring is like playing Russian roulette. Yet, if you properly formalize your procedure, it ceases to be a game of luck and provides you power of prediction!

Chapter

4

Formalize... or Die

"Otherwise smart people struggle to hire strangers. People unfamiliar to hiring methods consider the process a mysterious black art."

Steve Kerr, author of
"Reward Systems" [1]

WHEN SUBJECTIVITY RULES _____

Most employers seek to hire individuals who demonstrate obvious technical or administrative skills. Competencies are pretty easy to measure: you simply put the applicant to the test. You also want to hire people who are intelligent, articulate, responsible, have positive attitudes and who exercise initiative. How do you best detect those personality-related or behavioral skills, called soft skills?

This is where subjectivity comes in. The word "subjectivity" literally means: *"judgment based on individual personal impressions and feelings and opinions rather than external facts."*[2]

When it comes to measuring these soft skills in regard to a stranger, most small business owners and executives demonstrate poor judgment and evaluation aptitudes – especially when it needs to be done in less than an hour. More than often, subjectivity outweighs more objective criteria. There is nothing wrong with "feeling" good or bad about a candidate, except that those feelings are usually not valid when assessing job-related personality traits or behavioral characteristics.

Many studies have proven that the hiring decision is often made subconsciously within the first minute of meeting a candidate. The decision is mostly based upon the visual impact of the candidate. Per observation, the majority of employers tend to make most of their hiring assumptions before the candidate even opens his/her mouth! They will even judge factors such as intelligence, loyalty and honesty, based on an applicant's appearance. Also, most employers or managers will tend to hire people who have personality traits similar to their own.

Subjectivity is the big killer in hiring. Not only can "gut feelings" dramatically increase the risks of a bad or negligent hire; it also opens the door to employment discrimination. Subjective criteria are legally scrutinized because of the fear that they can be manipulated for a discriminatory purpose. Practically, it means that you could be sued by a rejected candidate for judging, for example, that his/her communication skills are insufficient for the applied-for position. Fortunately, you can protect yourself if you know how to "formalize" such subjective criteria.

Courts examining subjective hiring criteria are suspicious about their use, and have cautioned against their advancement because they can be easily fabricated. An employer can most probably defend a hiring or promotion decision based on subjective criteria, only to the degree that it can produce a factual basis for its assessment of the candidate. Some examples:

✓ In *Wingate v. Gage County School District*, the Eighth Circuit Court of Appeals ruled that an employer's use of subjective criteria did not create an inference of age discrimination when objective criteria were also utilized to make the employment decision.[3]

✓ In *Carter v. Three Springs Residential Treatment*, the Eleventh Circuit Court stated that the employer's requirements, such as the possession of "initiative and judgment capabilities" and the ability "to relate to people in a manner to win confidence and establish support" were incapable of objective evaluation. The plaintiff, an African-American, complained that he was rejected for a promotion in favor of a white individual. He lost the discrimination case.(4)

✓ In the age discrimination case, *Chapman v. Al Transport*, the 11th U.S. Circuit Court of Appeals ruled that an employer can successfully defend its employment decisions based on subjective reasons, as long as the employer can state a "reasonably specific factual basis" for its opinion.

The employer reportedly relied on its subjective determination that the plaintiff had interviewed poorly. But the company backed up its conclusion and satisfied the court's test by stating, among other things, that the individual was "not concise with his answers" and had not taken "an aggressive approach" in asking about the job.[5]

According to Section 30 of the Compliance Manual from the Department of Labor's Office of Federal Contract Compliance Program (OFCCP), employers utilizing subjective hiring criteria will be evaluated for disparate treatment based, in part, upon their use of "safeguards": [7]

"Safeguards consist of efforts made by the contractor to limit the possibility of differential application of the selection criteria/processes. In other words: treating members of a minority group or women differently than others in the application/evaluation of the criteria/processes. An example of a uniformly applied subjective process with safeguards could be an interview where all persons who pass the required test are interviewed regardless of minority or sex status; all interviewers are professionally trained in interviewing; all persons interviewed are asked the same questions; responses are documented; and answers are all evaluated in the same manner."

DID YOU KNOW?

In *Lockridge v. Board of Trustees of the University of Arkansas*, the Eighth Circuit concluded that employers who fail to establish "clear," objective selection procedures may open themselves to costly litigation — not only from existing employees and applicants, <u>but also from individuals who never even applied for a job</u>. In this case, Lockridge, an employee of the university, complained that his management should have offered him the job first, as he was qualified. He was not solicited.[6]

Minimizing subjectivity. The key to avoiding legal trouble, on top of risking the headaches, costs and frustrations attached to a bad hire, is to minimize subjectivity in your hiring process and to uniformly justify your subjective criteria. Specifically:

a.   Formalize your entire recruitment procedure. Make sure the same objective AND subjective selection criteria are used for <u>every applicant.</u>

b.   In every hiring and promotion decision, first assess the candidates' objective (not subjective), job-related skills and experience.

c.   Consider additional subjective criteria only if there is a clear and reasonably specific factual basis to support the subjective assessments. You must be able to show that they are directly job-related.

d.   Always document your assessments of candidates' objective and subjective qualifications.

e. Make desired soft skills explicit criteria in job descriptions. Clearly describe their job relatedness and business justification.

f. Assess whether each subjective criterion is creating an adverse impact, in which case you need to implement "safeguards" in the hiring process, described in the OFCCP Guidance.

How can you ascertain a factual basis for assessing job-related, but subjective, personality traits? How do you legally use important subjective criteria as formal part of your overall hiring procedure? Here are some hiring scenarios:

- You need an assertive, outgoing salesperson to take over a neglected area. You ask the candidate for an example of when he/she had to negotiate with tough customers and won the deal. You ask if there is any possibility of providing evidence of this. You then challenge the candidate in a "role playing" scenario where you are a tough customer. You take note of the candidate's answers to your question and reactions to the role playing.

- You want to hire a very creative person who will manage your design department. You ask the candidate to share some instances when he/she had to demonstrate creativity. You ask if there is any possibility of providing evidence of these. You then challenge the applicant with a problem which requires a fast, creative response. You take note of the candidate's answers to your question and reactions to the challenge.

- You are looking for a high-spirited sales manager who can motivate your sales team to fight harder in a very competitive environment. You ask the candidate to tell you about past experiences when he/she was able to inspire and manage salespeople in tough economic environments. You ask if there is any possibility of providing evidence of these. You then challenge the applicant with a specific problem regarding your sales team. You take note of his/her answers and reactions to the challenge.

In summary: Whatever the job and for every candidate, always standardize your subjective selection criteria evaluation during an interview, by doing the following:

1) Ask applicant to describe situations in which he/she exhibited the desired subjective trait(s)and ask for evidence,

2) Ask applicant to describe how he/she would carry out a task that requires the desired subjective trait(s).

3) Take precise notes at the end of the interview, stating to what extent the candidate exhibited the desired trait(s).

FORMALIZING YOUR JOB DESCRIPTION _____

A job description should be used as a formal and practical guide for hiring, staff planning, training, coaching and performance appraisal. It should help you sort out tasks, work flows and responsibilities, enabling you to plan how your company or even a specific job will operate and grow. But it is much more than just an administrative tool:

- A job description should first set a clear purpose for the job as well as clear performance expectations. According to Ferdinand Fournies in *"Why Don't Employees Do What They're Supposed to Do and What To Do About It,"* this is the first place to look if people aren't doing what you expect them to do.[8] Most job descriptions focus too much on tasks rather than being purpose-driven.

- Strategically, a well-developed job description provides an opportunity to clearly communicate your company direction and allows you to detect whether a future employee will fit or not with your business plans. Alignment with your goals and visions spells better chances of success for your organization.

- A job description serves as legal protection against potential discrimination complaints. It provides written evidence that your employment decisions were based on a rational, business-needs oriented, legal foundation.

- At the very beginning of your hiring process, it shows candidates what is expected of them and specifies minimum levels of acceptable job performance. It also satisfies a very human need: employees feel more comfortable and more confident when they know what you want and expect from them.

Each job opening must be developed in alignment with your job advertisement (see next chapter). We believe that the best way to write one is by answering the various questions most top players have when preparing themselves to meet a potential employer for an interview.

Content of a job description. After interviewing and surveying thousands of candidates, we found out that many candidates do not bother to learn about the exact content and boundaries of their job. On the other hand, we also found out that most qualified, top players have some precise questions regarding the vacant position.

You can develop the best job description by formally answering these questions. It will also make your life easier during the whole selection procedure:

1.   What is the exact title of the job?

2.   If applicable: in which division is this job located?

3.   To whom does the employee report?

4.   What is the importance of this division in the company activity and what will be its relative importance within the next 3 to 5 years?

5.   Is this job a new one or is it a vacancy due to a departure?

6.   What specific challenges are attached to this job?

7.   What products/services are directly or indirectly handled by the job?

8.   What is the targeted market for these products/services?

9.   What is the purpose of the job – how does it contribute to the purposes of the company?

10.   What are the precise performance/results expectations?

11.   How are those result expectations monitored and measured?

12.   What are the precise tasks, duties and responsibilities of the job?

13. What are the required technical competencies?

14. What is the desired or required experience?

15. How important is teamwork and coordination of efforts?

16. What are the required personality and behavioral characteristics? Why?

17. What impact could a good or a bad decision on the job have on the division and the company performance?

18. What management style applies to the supervision of the job?

19. What is the planned salary and other compensations?

20. What training program is planned for fast results achievement?

21. What kind of performance appraisal is planned on the job?

22. Does this job offer career development opportunities?

To see a few examples of job descriptions, visit www.nofailhiring.com.

Six steps to a great job description. Before you start your next hiring mission, you should be ready with its related job description. Never start hiring before developing it, as it would be suicidal both from quality and legal viewpoints. We suggest the following six steps:

1. Formalize the company's vision. Make sure the job description aligns well with the company vision, mission and strategic plans. Any qualified applicant will want to have an idea of "where you are going" and what the future looks like – a vital selection criterion for top players (see next chapter).

2. Involve the right people. Gather the concerned executives and/or employees who are connected to the position. Whoever the new employee will work with is the one who should provide the most relevant data.

3. Perform a detailed job analysis. What are the specific needs and requirements on that job? How was it held before? If this is a new post, how will you monitor and measure performance, etc? Use the questions provided in this book to do your analysis.

4. Write the actual job description. You can see a few examples at www. nofailhiring.com.

5. Review the description. Once the person is operational, review that job description periodically. Experience may lead to new, additional data and revised performance evaluation criteria.

6. Use it for your employee development plan. Your new employee's job description should be an integral part of his/her quarterly development plan or performance appraisal.

DID YOU KNOW?

An important feature we recommend to add in all your job descriptions is the special mention "... *and other duties as assigned.*" This allows you to add new tasks to the position as needed. You might include more specific tasks such as "other administrative duties," or "other duties as assigned by [a particular department of position]," etc. It also naturally leads employees to be more dedicated and less reluctant to do tasks that are not detailed in their job description but yet need to be done.

YOUR STANDARD JOB APPLICATION FORM

A standard job application form is one of the best pre-screening tools you can use, along with candidates' resumes. There are many standard job application forms – some of them free – you can download from the Internet. For example, U. S. Legal Forms™, Inc. provides state-specific, paid-for employment application and contract forms.[9] Be aware that many forms offered online might not actually be valid. A key point to successfully defending a discrimination claim based on failure to hire is being able to prove that you consistently evaluated all applicants using identifiable but legally acceptable criteria.

Important content: Some practical points must be considered in the development and use of your job application form. Without any pretenses of being complete or fully respectful of some state requirements, here are some tips on what you should include:

- All applicants must complete it without exception. Not doing so openly invites discrimination claims. Also, you may have difficulty in establishing consistency in your evaluation if not every applicant is required to fill out an application.

- Provide clear notice of employment conditions. Advance notice will help identify applicants who are not fully motivated. Also specify any particular, uncommon condition of employment (ex: trade secrets, drug testing, credit check, at-will status, etc.)

- Require that the applicant provides all his/her employment certifications, professional licenses and any other relevant qualifications for the job.

- The applicant should be required to sign a certification that the provided information is accurate and truthful.

- The form should request that the applicant indicates whether any current employer may be contacted for a reference.

- Clearly communicate that applicants are hired as "at-will" employees. Applicants will be more willing – and less surprised to accept without question or argument such terms of the employment relationship.

- Clearly state that any untruthfulness or gross omissions will automatically lead to the termination of the hiring process or employment, no matter when such things are discovered. This can be useful when an applicant was hiding a criminal conviction.

- Request the applicant's consent to pre-employment background screening, including academic and professional credentials, past employment and court records. Such a release may discourage an applicant who has something to hide.

- Ask about the applicant's social security number.

- Ask about past addresses (in California, limited to the last seven years). This helps in a criminal record search. You might also request that if employed, the applicant provide original identity documents or proof of right to work in the United States.

DID YOU KNOW?

Les Rosen, author of the excellent reference book, "*The Safe Hiring Manual,*" suggests that one of the best ways to check an applicant's criminal record is to formally ask the question in the application form. However, avoid the following three potentially dangerous mistakes in asking this question: [10]

1. **Too narrow** – An example is only to ask about felonies and not misdemeanors. An applicant could honestly state he/she was never convicted of a felony even though he/she was convicted of a serious misdemeanor you should know about.

2. **Too broad** - Some employers ask questions too broad to properly cover matters that are protected. If forced to say something defamatory about himself, an applicant may be able to file a lawsuit for defamation. For example, avoid asking: "please describe any act you have committed for which you could be punished by the law."

3. **Too ambiguous** – Asking questions that call for an opinion can lead the applicant to argue that in their mind, the offense was not serious and that their "no" answer was truthful. Do not ask "Did you commit serious misdemeanors" but rather "Did you commit misdemeanors?"

YOUR STANDARD RECRUITMENT
POLICY & GUIDELINE _____

<u>Remember</u>: the more standard the hiring process, the more objective your final decision and the less likely you will be a victim of discrimination retaliation. You must be able to demonstrate at any time that you fully abide by the EEOC and State employment regulations.

Keep in mind that some job seekers have become well-educated on the subject and a few might use the law to make "easy" money. There are enough hiring horror stories showing that it is being done, not just targeting big corporations but increasingly, small businesses as well.

Company hiring policy. Your full hiring process should be contained in a company policy that must be known by all executives and/or staff involved in hiring. It should contain the following elements (not exhaustive):

- You are an equal opportunity employer.

- Your employment-at-will statement.

- You have a person in charge of hiring – even if there is no human resource department in the company, who has been trained on hiring procedures.

- Your hiring "from within" preference statement.

- The use of a standard job application form for all applicants.

- Your personnel record keeping procedures.

- Your full adherence to EEOC regulations.

- Your exact hiring procedures and related documents.

- The rules and procedures regarding the use of reference checks and background checks on selected applicants.

- The rules regarding drug tests and medical examinations.

- Procedure related to the treatment of untruthful candidates.

- Statement about your employee referral program.

- Statement about hiring former employees.

To view an example of Company Hiring Policy, visit www.nofailhiring.com.

Company hiring guideline. A standard guideline helps you keep track of your hiring efforts and avoid confusion in the process. You can use it as a checklist as defined in your company hiring policy. You should always keep a copy of this guideline in each recruitment mission file.

Many of the steps presented below are covered in detail in subsequent chapters. The proposed sequence can be altered as per your specific needs and availabilities:

1. Define the real need for a new or replacement position.

2. Analyze the needed added value that the new hire will have to create in order to make the department or organization more productive.

3. Assess the financial and organizational consequences of the new hire with the direct supervisor/manager and the person in charge of hiring.

4. Gather all needed information on the job and its specific technical and/or administrative requirements.

5. Make up a list of skills/competencies and experience needed to successfully operate on the job.

6. Make up a list of all soft skills required or desired on the job.

7. Work out the salary range and other compensations for the job.

8. Develop a job description.

9. Post the opening internally. If you believe no one inside the company has the competencies to take the job, make sure you clearly post the required competencies so that everybody understands.

10. Simultaneously, start advertising the opening on your website, in specialty magazines, social media, etc. Do not wait for internal staff to apply if you believe none qualify.

11. Request that any interested internal applicant complete the standard job application form.

12. Ask each applicant who completes an application form to also sign a waiver and acceptance form related to reference and background checks. If applicable, do the same for drug tests and/or medical examinations.

13. Do a pre-screening on all received resumes and job applications (see chapter 6).

14. To select candidates to be interviewed, do a phone pre-screening with pre-selected applicants from point 13 above.

15. Send a courteous letter to all rejected applicants after you have completed the resume/job application and phone pre-screenings.

16. For all pre-selected, schedule a first interview with the person in charge of hiring or with direct supervisor.

17. Hold interviews with internal applicants. Make it clear that external applicants will also be interviewed if no internal applicant qualifies.

18. Conduct second interview with selected internal applicants.

19. If you decide to select an internal applicant, make a job offer.

20. If job offer is accepted with internal applicant, end the search.

21. If no job offer was done and/or accepted internally, continue the search and pre-selection process. You may want to expand your advertising efforts (next chapter).

22. Push your employee referral program (see next chapter).

23. Use all available external sources, web-based or not, to promote the job (see next chapter).

24. Continue the pre-screening process with incoming applications.

25. Schedule first interviews. If you invite an applicant who did not fill an application, always get him/her to complete it first.

26. Give each applicant a copy of the job description to be reviewed before the interview.

27. Keep documenting your interviews with each applicant. Make an application file for each. Do not write down any discriminatory or illegal notes which could lead to EEOC violations (see chapter 2 for what needs to be kept in an employee's or applicant file).

28. Make sure you ask the same questions of each applicant.

29. Make sure each applicant understands how specific, required soft skills are job-related and make it clear that the absence of any of these soft skills would justify termination of the application.

30. Make sure each applicant understands your hiring procedure and that the first interview is considered an in-depth pre-selection process.

31. At the end of the first interview, ensure that the applicant knows the details of the post as well as the proposed salary.

32. At the end of the first interview, fill out the applicant evaluation form. Do not postpone that vital action. If you wait too long, you will forget important details about specific soft skills.

33. Ensure that each applicant who has been pre-selected from the first interview has completed and fully signed the acceptance form regarding reference and background checks – and any other applicable search.

34. Coordinate with the direct supervisor or manager regarding who should be re-invited for a second interview, based on the applicant evaluation form and various checks.

35. Determine what other information needs to be obtained on an applicant, prior to meeting him/her for a second interview. Make a list on your applicant evaluation form.

36. Conduct reference checks prior to the second interview. See chapter 9 for further details.

37. Conduct the second interview with selected applicants. Use the second interview to challenge applicants on points uncovered during the first one, and through the different performed checks. See chapter 10 for further details.

38. Complete the applicant evaluation form for each interviewed applicant, adding the data obtained in the second interview. Make sure to ask the same questions to every selected applicant. See chapter 8 and 10 for a detailed list of questions.

39. Review selected applications with all concerned. Evaluate each finalist against required competencies and soft skills. Use the same standard skills and personality grid to score every one of them, ensuring that you can justify its job-relatedness.

40. Conduct background checks on selected applicants from the second interview. If you hire an external background check service company, make sure they comply with all applicable Fair Credit Reporting Act (FCRA) rules. See chapter 11 for further details.

41. Start sending proper letters of rejection to applicants who did not pass the second interview and/or background check steps.

42. Never justify an employment rejection with background check or interview results. Always limit your explanation to specifically observed disqualifying criteria during the whole selection process.

43. Confirm your interest with 3 to 4 applicants for each vacant job. This is not a job offer yet; you confirm your interest to offer a job, pending on some last details. Part of it is to informally discuss specifics of the employment relationship, covered during the second interview – reporting, salary and other conditions, etc.

44. Make it clear to finalists that employment remains conditional to background check results, even if they are hired prior to getting all of them. Employment offer remains contingent on obtaining acceptable feedback and results from those checks.

45. Work out the details of the employment relationship; formalize the salary with the preferred selected candidate. This may take place at the end of the second interview or later.

46. Formalize the job offer and the "at-will" agreement.

47. Schedule the start date with the new hire.

48. Complete sending of rejection letters to all other applicants. Keep some of them filed for possible hire later.

49. Keep two or three selected applicants in reserve, in case your first choice does not materialize into an employment agreement. If the above did not work out, repeat job offer with another pre-selected applicant.

50. If the mission did not provide a hire, review what went wrong, redefine the strategy and start again.

A last note: Remember that precise record keeping is important because it makes it easier to defend your case in discrimination lawsuits (see chapter 2). Choosing the longer administrative road in hiring will prove very beneficial to your company when a disappointed or frustrated applicant decides to take advantage of the many legal employment complexities against you!

NO-FAIL HIRING TIPS

- ⮑ Subjectivity is the killer in hiring. "Gut feelings" increase the risks of a bad or negligent hire. It also clearly opens the door to employment discrimination. You must be able to turn your subjective selection criteria into objective ones, mainly by proving their job-relatedness.

- ⮑ A well-developed job description might be your best "People Management" tool. It should also provide an opportunity to clearly communicate your company's direction and vision. On top of all, it serves as a legal protection against potential discrimination complaints.

- ⮑ To see examples of job descriptions, go to www.nofailhiring.com.

- ⮑ A standard job application form is a great pre-screening tool. It also helps you reduce discrimination claims, provided you demand ALL applicants complete the form.

- ⮑ Your hiring process should be contained in a company policy which demonstrates that you do not consider hiring a game of luck, but a strategically vital function that can deeply impact the viability of your business.

- ⮑ To see examples of a company hiring policy, go to www.nofailhiring.com.

- ⮑ Use a standard hiring guideline to help you keep track of your hiring efforts and avoid confusion in the process. On top of that, the guideline can serve as a legal protection in case of some discrimination claims.

- ⮑ We offer a series of unique templates and checklists as part of our *No-Fail Hiring™ System* training program. Go to www.nofailhiring.com for more information.

Whatever it takes to attract and hire the right people, it is never as painful and costly as having to dehire the wrong ones.

Chapter

5

The Hunt for Your Top Players

"For the foreseeable future, the 2 billion Web pages, tens of millions of candidates, and thousands of Web-based recruiting vendors will remain a swirling soup."

Michael Foster, author of *"Recruiting on the Web"* [1]

HOW TO PROMOTE YOUR JOB OPENINGS

Filling a job opening can take months of time and effort, depending on the required levels of qualification and experience. Considering the current economic conditions, applicants may take up to 6 months to find a job. Conventional wisdom is: 3 months for the first $50,000 of salary plus 1 month for every additional $10,000 in compensation desired.[2] However, you can speed up the process by smartly using a mix of available methods to promote a job opening.

Internal movements. Globally, hiring from within is still the most popular recruitment source for small businesses. A 2010 report by *CareerXRoads* reveals that over 51% of new jobs were offered to and taken by existing personnel.[3] The right talent might be hiding just under your nose. This trend will probably strengthen, as many companies work smarter to promote able employees tempted to look for a higher position with the competition.

Personal contacts/referrals. Most jobs are never advertised. Employee referral is still the most frequently used external recruitment method and by far the most efficient one. Next to internal promotion, talking openly with your employees, suppliers, customers or friends is the cheapest and most profitable way to fill a vacant job. Per *CareerXRoads*, it represents 27% of all external hires and 13% of all hires. The yield for referrals is one hire for every 15 referrals. [3]

Company career websites. Your website is a key tool for hiring, either as an information channel or a direct recruitment medium. In fact, all sources of hiring are dependent on your Web presence. No talented applicant will trust your business if the job opening is not posted via your Internet sources – starting with a job opening page. Per *CareerXRoads*, corporate websites represent 22.3% of external hires and 13.1% of all hires.[3]

Classified ads. Posting a good "Help Wanted" advertisement in newspapers and/or the Internet is the second most frequently used method of advertising job openings. A study by *yourwebfuture.com* reveals that very small businesses still favor printed classified ads to the Internet or private agencies. Barely 6% of very small firms (less than 50 employees) use online recruitment advertising. The aggressive use of the Internet is more common among "larger" small firms, with about 14% with 51 to 100 employees indicating frequent use of the Internet as a recruitment method. [4]

Job boards. The Internet includes many job hunting websites with job listings. Some job boards provide national listings of all kinds; others are local. Some relate to a specific type of work; others are general. *CareerBuilder.com* and *Monster.com* accounted for over 57% of all hires in this category. For financial reasons, job boards are not appreciated by small businesses which prefer the convenience of more conventional hiring promotional actions. Per *CareerXRoads*, job boards represented 13.2% of external hires and 6.5% of all hires in 2009. [3]

Private employment agencies and career consultants. Private agencies can save you time as they have access to thousands of job seekers. Such agencies may be called recruiters, head hunters, or employment placement agencies. Most charge a percentage of the first-year salary paid to a successful applicant. Find out the exact cost before using the service. When determining if the service is worth the cost, consider any guarantees that the agency offers. Ask for guarantees that your hired angels will not get solicited by that same agency at the end of the first year. Many agencies keep collected resumes alive for years.

School career planning and placement offices. High school and college placement services help their students and alumni find jobs. Some invite recruiters to use their facilities for interviews or career fairs. They also may have lists of open jobs. Most also offer career counseling, career testing, and job search advice.

Some have career resource libraries that host workshops on job search strategy, resume writing, letter writing and effective interviewing. They also critique drafts of resumes, conduct mock interviews and sponsor job fairs. Get yourself invited by the major high schools and colleges in your area. Networking with soon-to-be graduates is a sure way to attract them once they are on the job market.

Professional associations. Your membership with business-related professional associations will allow you to promote your employment opportunities through career planning, educational programs, job listings and job placements.

State employment service offices. State employment services, some-times called the Job Service, operate in coordination with the U.S. Depart-ment of Labor's Employment and Training Administration. Local offices, found nationwide, help job seekers to find jobs and help employers to find qualified workers at no cost to either. To find the office nearest you, look in the State government telephone listings under "Job Service" or "Employment."

Community agencies. Many nonprofit organizations, including reli-gious institutions and vocational rehabilitation agencies, offer counseling, ca-reer development and job placement services, generally targeted to a particu-lar group, such as women, youths, minorities, ex-offenders or older workers.

Internships. Many people find jobs with businesses and organizations with whom they have interned or volunteered. By offering internships to young people, you increase your chances of an effective internal hiring later. Post your internship opportunities on job boards, school career centers, and company websites.

HOW TO GET MORE FOR YOUR JOB AD BUCK

No matter what kind of paper or online media you use, you want your job opening ad to attract those who can be evaluated against our definition of "Top Players." The most important criteria are not just about competencies, but also and mostly about vital soft skills.

Writing an effective job ad is like writing any other kind of advertisement. The job is your product; the applicants are your potential customers. A job advertise-ment should follow the classical *"AIDA"* marketing format: *Attention, Interest, De-sire* and *Action.* This means that good job advertisements must first attract attention (from qualified job-seekers); raise interest (by establishing relevance in these quali-fied applicants' mind); create desire (to pursue what looks like a great opportunity) by delivering a strong message; and finally provide clear instructions for the next action or response. You need to direct applicants through a strong call to action.

When doing online job advertising, make sure you differentiate the job summary from the job advertisement itself. In this case, the job summary is a teaser. Use it to sell the available opportunity with the AIDA formula above. Once you have enticed them in to click on and read your full advertisement, you can provide them with more details about your organization and what you are offering.

The best way to learn how to write a great job advertisement is to find 8 to 10 ads online and in papers which you really like; find out why you like them and see how they are structured and follow the same pattern. Visit www.no-failhiring.com to access an example of a job advertisement checklist.

Note: Before you develop your recruitment ad, make sure you have created your full job description. It will make this part easier!

That being said, there are a few vital components of your recruitment ad that you cannot afford to neglect. Remember, you want to attract only potential top players. These qualified applicants respond to specific messages. Make sure you tell them what they want to read in order to be willing to follow up and talk to you:

Company information

- **Who you are**. A key factor in attracting top players is to "make it personal." Never forget that before people decide to join a company they have to be closed on its management team. People do not work for companies, they work for people. Do not underestimate this vital aspect of "people marketing."

- **What you do.** Describe your activities in terms of servicing a specific market, rather than just in terms of producing the best product or service. People may be interested in dealing with great products but top players are more excited to deal with people. Focus on how customers benefit from your services.

- **Where you are going.** Top players want to know what your vision is and what the future looks like. This is critical. Remember, a good applicant buys the future. If you can't sell the future, you will NOT attract top players.

- **Challenges.** This is a major keyword. Sell them your challenges, not job security. Do not be afraid to mention any challenge or difficulty related to the future of the business and also to the function – top players will love it and others will fear it. This is called natural selection.

DID YOU KNOW?

✓ It is more effective to publish a small ad several times, rather than publishing a large ad once. Message repetition gives more results, because it reaches more applicants. Therefore, plan a budget over several weeks.

✓ Do not hesitate to put your ad in various media. For example, any specialized press is often an effective means of attracting experienced applicants. Find out what media they read and use those to attract them to your website.

✓ Directing your readers to your website hiring page is the best technique you can use. It is highly recommended to dedicate one page per vacant job on your website, where you do not pay for space. It also allows you to be more specific and to provide the needed details as presented above.

✓ If you have a very limited budget, minimize your paper advertisement expenses and increase your web-based budget. 92% of qualified applicants will not consider you are a serious employer if you are not promoting your job opening(s) on the Internet. Use teasers on the paper media and develop your actual ad on your dedicated website page.

Job information

- **Expected results & performance**. As mentioned in the previous chapter, no matter what the job is, you must have a way of monitoring and evaluating performance. If you can't define what results are expected on a job, that job should not exist! Unfortunately, many people do not think in terms of results but mostly in terms of action – and thus need direction. If you have room for only one piece of information about the job in your ad, it should be about expected results.

- **Responsibilities and duties.** The applicant should understand what he/she is expected to do on a daily basis. Focus on the responsibilities in terms of contribution to the company's results and customer satisfaction, more than just on activities.

- **Personal profile.** What professional background, experience and attitude do you require on that specific job? Remember to focus more on soft skills than technical ones. Tell them what kind of people you want to work with. If you expect a new hire to smile, tell them why; if you want them to be courteous, tell them why. Be specific in describing what kind of personality is needed to be successful on the specific job.

<u>Other important information</u>

- **Rewards/benefits.** Do not hesitate to give *some* information on the salary and other compensations. Providing a salary range is a good way to make things clear from the very beginning and avoid wasting any time during the interview.

- **The "caring" factor.** People want to know that you will provide attention, support and basic training to help them perform fast, once on the job. They also want to see what you are willing to do to make them more competent.

- **How to apply.** What do you want them to do next: send a resume or cover letter? Apply online? Clearly communicate how to apply and provide contact information.

- **Relevant keywords.** Use keywords to ensure your job opening can be found on Google, Yahoo, Career Builder and other niche sites. Think from the job seeker's perspective about words they would search that describe the position they may be looking for.

DID YOU KNOW?

You could be charged for discrimination by just posting a job advertisement. Ensure your ad copy adheres to employment regulatory standards to avoid discrimination cases.

For example: You should not ask for specific amounts of experience or a specific academic degree level without the words "*or equivalent.*" This applies to both paper and online messages.

- **Keep it short, simple and sweet.** What reaction would you have to a six or seven page resume? The same holds true with job seekers. Less than 20% of job seekers read job postings word-by-word; keep yours to one or two pages, ideally.

A last note: if you pay a communication agency to develop your recruitment ad, ask them to read this chapter first.

THE EVER-GROWING POWER OF SOCIAL NETWORKS

Online job boards seem to be losing out to social media when companies search for new employees. Today, nearly three-quarters of companies use social networks for recruiting and say they have successfully hired a candidate through a social network.

Success in this area is leading almost half of all employers to increase recruiting program spending on social media. At the same time, more than a third of all companies were lowering spending on job boards and search firms. While the economy begins to recover, companies looking to make new hires are indeed seeking the most cost-effective, efficient ways to find new talent. Per Dan Finnigan, president and CEO of *Jobvite*:

"Job boards launched a revolution in recruiting more than 15 years ago; now social networks are doing the same – but in a targeted way. Through social recruiting, companies are learning they can find the best talent efficiently, without making a major investment."[5]

A new kind of background & reference checks. Companies are increasingly using social media to evaluate applicants' potential fits. According to a recent poll by *Digital Brand Expressions* and *Interbiznet*, as many as 75% of employers use *LinkedIn* on a regular basis to research candidates before making an offer, compared to 48% using *Facebook*, and 26% using *Twitter*.

DID YOU KNOW?

By June 2010, *LinkedIn* was the top social network looked to for hiring, used by nearly 80% of companies recruiting through social media. It also provided the most success, with about 90% of companies who had hired through a social network reporting they found the candidate on LinkedIn.

While *Facebook* and *Twitter* were used for recruiting by about 55% and 45% of companies, respectively, they led to far fewer hires: 27.5% for *Facebook* and 14.2% for *Twitter*.[6]

"Social media is not only a great networking tool, it's also a way for employers to perform reference checks on job candidates," says Veronica Fielding, president of *Digital Brand Expressions* and its social media service for consumers, *Jump Start Social Media.* [7]

These social networks tend to attract employers and hiring managers for doing due diligence. Access to an applicant's personal information is often easy and can be used to do background checks.

Mark Presnell, director of Career Center at *Johns Hopkins* in Maryland, advises students to create a profile in *LinkedIn* because having some presence in social media enhances their chances of finding success or internship. Presnell further advises his students:

"Keep your professional experience on LinkedIn and keep your personal experience on Facebook. Preferably do not use Facebook for social networking with employers and keep your Facebook settings private. Be conscious of the content; think about what information you want others to see."[8]

According to a study commissioned by *CareerBuilder.com*, 45% of companies use social networking sites to research job candidates, while an additional 11% are planning to implement social media screening in the very near future. Per that same study, 35% of employers reported they have found content on social networking sites that caused them not to hire the screened candidates, while 18% of them found content that led them to hire applicants.[9]

A note of caution: Employers ought to be careful not to attract employment legislation inspectors or to open the door to discrimination cases. There are potential legal problems linked to looking at an individual's personal information through sites like *Facebook* or other social media. Our advice:

- When checking for an applicant online, make sure you keep your evaluation criteria directly related to professional considerations. Do not write anything in your files about a potential candidate who was rejected before he/she could even talk to you. The best is to limit your search to *LinkedIn*, which is 100% professional or business related.

- Don't give an applicant the chance to complain with the EEOC because he/she was disqualified based on your investigation of his/her *Facebook* or other social media profile. We predict that such cases will soon bloom as discrimination lawyers will find new ways of prosecuting discrimination cases.

DID YOU KNOW?

Per *CareerBuilder.com*, the main reasons why companies reject an applicant after evaluating his/her social media profile are: [9]

- Provocative or inappropriate photographs or information – **53%**

- Content showing applicant drinking or using drugs – **44%**

- Bad-mouthed previous employer, co-workers or clients – **35%**

- Poor communication skills – **29%**

- Discriminatory comments – **26%**

- Lied about qualifications – **24%**

- Shared confidential information from previous employer – **20%**

A NEW LOOK AT EMPLOYEE REFERRAL PROGRAMS

Employee referrals have always been the first and most effective source of hires. As many as 75% of placements are done through networking. Hiring an employee's friend, relative or even a simple acquaintance is proven to be cheaper than going through the whole costly chain of a hiring mission.

Having spent over a decade advising staffing leaders and reviewing the performance of hundreds of staffing organizations across the country, Dr. John Sullivan, Professor of Management at San Francisco State University and the so-called "Michael Jordan of Hiring" by *Fast Company magazine*, states:

> *"I can attest that when managed well, no other sourcing channel can come remotely close to producing the results of a good employee referral program."* [10]

Depending on the size of your hiring needs, you might also want to explore online employee referral services. Until recently, only big employers were relying on referral services as a way to spot great candidates. Now the trend seems to catch employers of all sizes.

An online referral service is an e-mail job distribution method paid for by employers. It helps job seekers identify which of their contacts may know people at the companies where they want to work.

A number of services pay a fee to referrers — company employees or trusted outsiders acting as amateur recruiters — when a hire is made. The typical fee is $500 to $3,000 or more. Some online recruiting services pay no fees to referrers. Examples of online referral services are Jobvite.com, Jobster. com and Selectminds.com, all of which are free for subscribing job seekers.

Cash for referrals. More and more, companies of all sizes are making employee referral THE source of their search for talent, arguing that the associated costs are always much less than recruiting through classic channels – and it brings in better workers. Some examples: [11]

- **Intel Corp.** The computer hardware giant uses a combination of monetary and nonmonetary incentives to get employees to refer others. In 2009, the prize was a choice between a $1,000 travel voucher and a home-entertainment system. About 50 percent of the company's new hires come from referrals.

- **Brooktrout Inc.** The electronic communications firm gets 37% of its hires from employee referrals. After their referral has been on the job for 90 days, employees get a whopping $3,000 check. The employee-referral program is "a lot more economical than an agency," according to sources.

- **BioTek Instruments Inc.** The company awards $2,000 for new senior-level-employee referrals and $1,000 for those hired at the developer level. The new employee has to be on the job for 30 days before the worker gets the referral reward. BioTek Instruments also has a friend-of-a-friend referral program, in which employees receive either $1,000 or $500 for naming a potential job candidate they don't know personally.

DID YOU KNOW?

Per Hans Gieske, former president of Monster.com, offering money for referrals will not corrupt your employees' motivation. More than about money, it's first of all about helping people who are important to them.

Though it's not all about the money, creating the "right" referral reward is quite important. Employees/people who make referrals have a pretty good idea how much money they're saving the employer. Five to ten percent of the annual salary seems to work best. Offering a wrong reward is worse than asking for free referrals, says Gieske. [12]

- **Satyam Computer Services Ltd.** The IT consulting and services provider with offices in the U.S. and India gets about 26 percent of new hires from employee referrals. The company offers between $500 and $1,000 for a referral, and some corporate bigwigs also give rewards like cars and iPods to those who nab workers with unique and sought-after skills.

Simple rules for success. What does it take to run and operate an effective employee referral program? The basic rules are simple:

a. Make it part of the company's philosophy to invite employees to bring their friends and acquaintances. Formalize the program through a company policy.

b. Make a suggestion to trusted employees to develop their profile on LinkedIn and to informally inform their contact base of any job opening, with a link to your company job opening web page.

c. Educate your employees on the program. Make it clear that it has the purpose of ensuring the best hiring picks, which will profit everyone.

d. It is not just about bringing friends in, it is mostly about attracting top players. Share the job description and the ad so your employees understand exactly what you are looking for.

e. It does not need to be about money. Recognition and formal acknowledgement are sometimes more valuable. But rewarding with a cash prize will motivate employees to do it again. We advise to offer a "start" bonus and a bigger one once the new employee has shown real performance after a specific period.

f. Put someone in charge to push the referral program. If you don't have anyone consistently asking for referrals, you won't get any. It can be anybody in the company who will get rewarded with anyone who brings in a top player. Invite that person to develop skills on how to use social networks for referral programs.

g. Do not compromise on your hiring procedure because an applicant was referred by an employee. You do not want to be accused of discrimination or allow subjectivity to prevail. Use the same standard hiring procedure, no matter who applies.

The real key to a successful referral program is to make it part of your business strategy. Keep it alive by consistently motivating your employees to be involved. The key is to get everybody excited about building an effective team and to communicate how hiring top talent leads to job security and improved company performance.

NO-FAIL HIRING TIPS

○ You can speed the process of attracting and hiring top players by smartly using the mix of available methods to promote a job opening. Don't stick to the classic ones.

○ Your company website is a key tool for hiring, either as an information channel or as a direct recruitment medium. All sources of hiring actually depend on your Web presence. Make sure both your webmaster and your communication agency are well-coordinated to make the job description fit with your job summary.

○ When it comes to writing an effective job ad, remember it is like writing any kind of advertisement. The job is your product; the applicants are your potential customers. Make sure that you communicate to attract top players, not job security seekers. Use the list of vital information as presented in this chapter to develop your advertisement.

○ Even if social networking is not yet heavily used in the world of small businesses, you want to take advantage of its impressive uptrend to attract top players. These individuals understand the value of being connected and will definitely favor employers who are themselves communicating in the virtual world.

○ Be careful if you check an applicant's profile on any social media. Ideally limit your search to LinkedIn, which is 100% professional information-based. Do not invite discrimination retaliation for openly rejecting applicants based on his/her online social profile.

○ Employee referral is still the most frequently used external recruitment method and by far the most efficient one. Make it a formal part of your business strategy; turn your employees into volunteer headhunters – and reward them for helping you find top players.

Part B

The
Selection
Process

The pre-selection process requires some investigative talent. It can either be an exciting step to finding your top players or the start of your worst nightmares.

Chapter

6

Your Best Pre-Selection Strategy

"The most expensive person you'll ever hire is the one you have to fire."

Mel Kleiman, author of
"Hire Tough – Manage Easy" [1]

VALUE AND LIABILITY OF RESUMES _____

Can you trust a resume? You have started to collect resumes from your recruitment promotion campaigns. Depending on the job and your promotional efforts, you may receive less than 10 or more than 100 resumes. Remember, for every currently available job in the U.S., there are 5.6 people looking for one.

How much can you rely on resumes to implement a formal pre-selection process? It is a well-known fact that most applicants today have access to professional resume consultants or online templates. According to the independent investigative firm, *Market International LTD*, one-third of resumes contain material omissions or misstatements of one kind or another.[2] Other alarming statistics warn us of the questionable reliability of resumes:

- An *Automatic Data Processing* (ADP) 2009 study of some 5.5 million background investigations showed discrepancies in 46% of educational, employment and/or reference checks, up from 45% in 2008 and 41% in 2007.[3]

- According to *CareerBuilder.com*, although just 5% of workers admitted to fibbing on their resume, 57% of hiring managers say they have caught a lie on a candidate's application. Of those who spotted the lie, 93% did not hire the candidate.[4]

- A 2004 Society for Human Resources Management survey of personnel directors found that nearly 90% reported that they had been subjected to resume fraud and that 61% had found inaccuracies.[5]

- ADP's 2001 survey of some 2.3 million background checks concluded that 44% of job applicants lied about their work histories; 41% lied about their educational backgrounds; and 23% falsified credentials or professional licenses.[6]

- A 2001 study of 7,000 resumes assembled by *Christian & Timbers* found that nearly 25% contained at least one instance of the job applicants misrepresenting their credentials.[7]

Screening a resume. Does it mean that resumes should be banned from your inventory of pre-screenings checks on applicants? Absolutely not! We believe that a resume can be a fantastic indicator or challenger of honesty, consistency and adequacy, IF you know how to analyze one. First of all, you need to know where most instances of untruthfulness occur.

Potential "lie detector" points of a resume:

1) Hiding employment gaps by altering dates

2) Lying about academic degrees

3) Listing a degree from a school never attended

4) Omitting graduation dates to appear younger

5) Exaggerating performance numbers

6) Inflating previous or current salary

7) Embellishing job title, to get a better salary

8) Providing an incorrect reason for leaving a previous job

9) Exaggerating a technical ability

10) Claiming some foreign language fluency

11) Providing fake addresses

12) Omitting past employment

13) Supplying fraudulent references

The second step in a resume analysis (whether paper or electronic form) is to spot specific points of qualification and interest against the job description. You may use a checklist similar to the following. We strongly suggest that you attach such checklist to each resume with answers "yes," "+/-" or "no" clearly noted. This will provide quality and legal weight to the formalization of your pre-screening process.

Checklist for a resume screening:

✓ A personalized cover letter is attached to resume.

✓ Resume is job-specific rather than generic (same resume sent to multiple employers).

DID YOU KNOW?

You should warn applicants that lying on a resume or application form will lead to automatic termination of application or employment. Many companies have done so. Here are a few examples, as reported by the Wall Street Journal: [8]

- Gregory Probert, President of Herbalife Ltd., lost his job in 2008 after the Wall Street Journal disclosed that his corporate biography listed a fake master's degree.

- Tetra Tech Inc. demoted its president, Sam Box, after he acknowledged he hadn't earned the bachelor's degree he had been claiming.

- Cabot Microelectronics Corp. forced its Chief Information Officer, James Dehoniesto, to leave the company after it discovered that he had claimed a fake bachelor's degree.

✓   The main education is relevant and sufficient for the job.

✓   There is additional relevant educational experience.

✓   The education is relatively current.

✓   Resume shows acceptable professional experience (if applicable) enabling applicant to be quickly operational on the job.

✓   Resume covers required job requirements stated in the ad.

✓   Resume shows main relevant points of qualification.

✓   The timeline throughout the resume is consistent and does not contain unexplained "gaps" in the job history and/or education.

✓   Resume shows congruence of information– no omitted dates, descriptions, references, etc.

✓   Applicant's job history shows consistent, stable career path.

✓   Resume shows performance/achievement data.

✓ Professional experience is given in terms of results, rather than just in terms of action/tasks.

✓ Applicant's background seems compatible with company culture and management style.

✓ Resume shows applicant's involvement in volunteer activities.

✓ Resume contains soft skills that are important for the job.

✓ Applicant presents verifiable references or testimonials.

✓ Applicant mentions salary range compatible with job pay.

✓ The general appearance of resume is professional.

✓ Overall, resume appears credible.

Note: beware of "functional" resumes. They ignore chronological order and focus on skills and capabilities — what the applicant can do rather than what he/she has done. The functional format is usually used by those who have unexplained gaps in employment, have changed careers over the years or have unclear career paths. The only interest in analyzing a functional resume is for new graduates who don't have much professional experience.

PRE-SCREENING FROM THE JOB APPLICATION

As mentioned earlier, we strongly suggest using both an applicant's resume and job application for pre-screening purposes. A standard job application form offers the following advantages:

- It can provide your company with legal protection during and after the hiring process.

- A standard application form avoids receiving illegal information from applicants, whereas a resume may contain personal information unsuitable for hiring purposes.

- Your standard application form allows you to quickly pre-screen many candidates, as you analyze the same criteria for each of them. Resumes lack uniformity, which could lead to claims of disparate treatment.

- Missing information on a job application is obvious. A resume does not always provide all the requested data.

- A standard application is easier to scan for any gaps in an applicant's job history.

- You can add your legal protection clauses in the application form (see chapter 4).

Remember, your application form should also contain a space where the applicant can sign, certifying that the information provided is true and acknowledging that inaccurate statements can lead to rejection of their application, or if employed, to termination of their employment.

While many experts recommend ignoring resumes and working only with applications, scanning a resume also offers advantages:

- It shows information not available on a standard form.

- It provides data on soft skills in a more useful manner.

- It may help reveal inconsistency and gaps.

- Even if done with the help of a professional, it may reflect the applicant's personality better.

- The cover letter usually tells more about the applicant.

- The structure of a resume may, to some degree, indicate the applicant's analytical level.

Screening a job application. You may use a checklist similar to the following. As with resume screening, we strongly suggest that you attach such a checklist to each resume with answers "yes," "+/-" or "no" clearly noted. Each pre-selected applicant folder will thus contain two checklists.

Checklist for job application screening:

1) Application is complete without blanks, gaps or omissions.

2) The main education is relevant and sufficient for the job.

3) There is additional relevant educational experience.

4) Application shows acceptable professional experience (if applicable), enabling applicant to be quickly operational on the job.

5) Application covers the required job requirements as stated in the advertisement or job description.

6) Application shows main relevant points of qualification.

7) The timeline throughout the application is consistent and does not contain unexplained "gaps" in the applicant's job history and/or education.

8) Application shows congruence of information – no omitted dates, descriptions, references, etc.

9) Applicant has given social security number.

10) Application provides performance/achievement data.

11) Presents professional experience in terms of results, rather than just in terms of action/tasks.

12) Applicant's background seems to reflect compatibility with company culture and management style.

13) Application shows applicant's involvement in volunteer or community activities.

14) Application contains soft skills that are important for the job.

15) Applicant presents verifiable references or testimonials.

16) Applicant mentions salary range compatible with job pay.

17) Application was completed neatly and orderly.

18) Overall, application appears credible.

Additional important check points:

19) Application is signed by the applicant.

20) Applicant signed consent to reference/background checks.

21) Applicant has signed consent for drug or medical testing.

22)   Answer to question about criminal record is negative or,

23)   If answer to question about criminal record is positive, clear data is provided – leaving no mystery or suspicion.

24)   Applicant has provided accurate data on past employers.

25)   Applicant has provided clear reason for leaving a past job and/ or for seeking new employment.

26)   Application appears compatible with resume data.

Detection of "red flags." Besides serving its first and most vital purpose of providing qualification data, a job application is (together with the resume) a great investigation tool.

You can deepen your screening process by cross-checking both resume and application checklists to detect eight "dangerous indicators" of a potential bad hire or legal trouble.

<u>"Red flag" indicators from resume and application:</u>

1)   Unexplained gaps appear in applicant's job history.

2)   Unexplained omissions are detected in document timeline.

3)   No references or past employer data is provided.

4)   Applicant completed but did not sign job application.

5)   Applicant did not sign consent to background check.

6)   Applicant left the criminal record blank.

7)   Applicant failed to give clear explanation for leaving past job.

8)   Applicant failed to provide social security number.

ONLINE PRE-SCREEENING

The main objective with pre-screening actions is to differentiate your potential top players from unqualified applicants. The purpose of online pre-screening is to automate and speed up the pre-selection process. If you post your job advertisement online, you have the option to use online pre-screening services.

DID YOU KNOW?

Many well-known organizations have learned the importance of verifying employees' credentials and background the hard way. Here are a few examples showing the dangers/liabilities of resume fraud. Make sure it does not happen to you:

- In 2006, RadioShack was publicly embarrassed after it was revealed their newly-appointed CEO, David Edmondson, had not earned the education credentials he claimed.[9]

- In 2006, George Deutsch, a NASA public affairs officer appointed by President George W. Bush, resigned when it was discovered he had not completed the bachelor's degree he had always claimed.[10]

- In 2002, it was revealed that Kenneth Lonchar, then CFO of Veritas Software, had not earned a Stanford University MBA degree as he had claimed. In the wake of this revelation, Lonchar resigned and the company's stock price fell about 14.4%.[11]

If you plan a minimum of 10 new hires per year, we believe it is worth creating your own online pre-screening. You can have your job announcement page provide a link to an electronic job application form. A good programmer can help prioritize the important qualification criteria and provide you with an automated version of your manual checklists.

On the other hand, there are many specialized companies offering advanced online pre-screening and testing services. Depending on the specifics of the vacancy and its relative importance to your company's development, these services vary as follows:

- **Basic screening.** This system automatically evaluates the match between the job seeker's qualifications and a job's requirements. It ranks the most qualified applications at the top.

- **Technical skills assessment.** This system uses testing software that requires applicants to prove their knowledge and skills in a specific area of expertise. Online skill testing is especially useful in technical or information technology jobs where dealing with computer-assisted equipment or software is important.

- **IQ testing.** IQ tests can be administered for important functions.

- **Personality assessment.** Using personality testing as a pre-screening tool is not advised. Attempts to measure work-related personality traits to predict job success is one of the more controversial types of online testing.

   As we will see in the next chapter, personality traits are important only if they are proven to be related to job success. Using personality tests too early in the process can lead to biased opinions as many of them do not provide accurate, realiable information.

- **Performance-based assessment.** Challenges applicants about past, demonstrable performance in specific fields, compatible with or similar to the vacant job.

- **Behavioral assessment.** Challenges applicants on precise soft skills required by your company to be successful and effective on the specific job.

- **Managerial assessment.** Challenges applicants with typical managerial scenarios and asks them to react. It is typically an electronic multiple-answers questionnaire.

Our position. A good online pre-screening instrument should be entirely job-based and fair to all people with equal skills. An applicant would survive the first screening step, based on his/her technical or administrative ability to perform on the job.

On the negative side, the use of an online process is automated and devoid of human evaluation. As mentioned earlier, soft skills are the scarcest and most important criteria of success for most jobs; it is also the first reason why employers are unhappy with staff.

Our recommendation. Use a well-proven online pre-screening system that is flexible enough to provide you with the compiled data without automatic, "blind" elimination, based on lack of competencies or experience. Those pre-eliminated applicants could well be your best top players, once you analyze their soft skills – which can only be done effectively through smart interview and selection process (see PART 3, THE DECISION PROCESS).

A note on external screening companies. A good reason to work with them is that a dependable screening service company has a better likelihood of going through the process legally. It also gives more assurance of completeness. An incomplete search can be devastating to both you and an applicant. For example, if an applicant were a victim of criminal identity theft, the report could include criminal records that are not his/hers.

If you plan to hire an outside screening service company for employment purposes, note that the Fair Credit Report Act (FCRA) requires you, the employer, to provide the following information to the reporting agency:

- Verify that you are legitimately investigating an applicant.
- Certify that you have obtained permission from the applicant.
- State the reason that you are requesting the report.
- Certify that the data will only be used for employment purposes.

Selection of a screening service provider. As an employer, you also deserve some assurance that the screening process actually reveals vital information that could be potentially harmful to your company – and is legal. Before you decide to establish a relationship with a screening firm, verify the following points:

1) Does it follow the FCRA and applicable laws?

2) Does it provide the right guidance about your responsibilities?

3) Does it provide forms to obtain permission from applicants and does it give them the required notice?

4) Does it guide you in case of an "adverse action" decision?

5) Does it provide applicants access to reports and to their files?

6) Does it follow legal procedures for investigating inaccurate data?

PHONE SCREEENING

Phone screening is your best second level of investigation. Once you have narrowed your stack of applications to a handful of potential applicants, call them and use your phone screening questions to further narrow the field. Using a consistent set of questions will help ensure you are evaluating candidates consistently.

A telephone screening is a short phone conversation (typically 20 to 30 minutes) that delves into an applicant's qualifications to a higher level. Your objective is to determine or challenge whether a pre-selected candidate has the requisite skills and qualifications you are looking for, and if it is worthwhile to grant them an interview.

It is important to outline 5 to 10 standard questions that can provide you with additional information on the applicant's profile. Call each qualified candidate. Take notes on a standard phone screening report form.

Grade the candidates on the quality of their responses and their interest in the position. You can use a numerical rating of 1 to 10 for each answer. This helps minimize the subjectivity of your evaluation.

Purposes of a phone interview. Consider a phone screening action as a formal interview. Thus some questions should never be asked (see chapter 10). A phone screening action has four purposes:

1) To clarify or challenge some qualifications presented in the resume and/or application.

2) To "set the rules of the game" regarding the whole selection process.

3) To establish some relationship in order to determine if the applicant possesses some important, job-related soft skills.

4) To be able to assess, at the end of the phone interview, if an "face-to-face" interview is justified.

Phone screening questions. Here is a suggested list of questions to ask. It is not an exhaustive list. We also recommend that you have your phone screening script reviewed by your employment attorney, as specific State laws may vary.

1) Our job advertisement mentions clearly some required specific skills and competencies. Can you tell me what they are?

2) How did you develop such skills and competencies?

3) Can you give me examples when you had to demonstrate such skills and competencies?

4) Why do you believe your background and experience will match this job better than someone else?

5) (If application revealed gaps in applicant's job history) What did you do between [date] and [date]?

6) *If points 19 to 25 of the application form were left unclear (see checklist for job application screening earlier in this chapter), clarify now.*

7) We systematically perform formal background and credit checks as well as criminal checks prior to making a job offer. Do you have any concern about such a procedure?

8) We also systematically perform reference checks by contacting applicants' former employers. What feedback should we expect from each of them?

Important notes:

- Ask the same questions to every applicant. If you need to clarify a specific point with a "unique" question, note down on your phone screening report form why you asked that question. This will help you justify the question later, in case of inquiry from someone else (e.g., the rejected applicant's lawyer).

- Specify the 3 to 4 soft skills vital for the job and focus on evaluating these during the phone interview. List these soft skills on the phone screening report form and evaluate each of them at the end of the phone interview.

- You can also grade "standard" attributes expected from every applicant on the phone (excellent, good, fair, poor):

  - courteousness and manners,

  - level of communication,

  - interest for the position,

  - enthusiasm in answering the questions,

  - spontaneity (or lack of) in answering questions,

  - reaction to background and reference questions.

- Whatever the outcome of the phone interview, explain the next step(s) in the process to the applicant prior to hanging up. If you decided not to invite the applicant for a "face-to-face" interview, do not tell the applicant now. Simply explain that you are interviewing a number of other candidates and that the next step will be decided once all applicants have been contacted and interviewed.

DID YOU KNOW?

Pre-screening candidates from resumes/applications and on the phone can be done by a trusted, internally-trained person. Spare your time as business owner to meet selected applicants personally. Ideally you should only see those who passed the first interview as well as any specific testing. See PART 3, THE DECISION PROCESS.

NO-FAIL HIRING TIPS

➲ Don't underestimate the value of a resume but be aware of its limits. When well-analyzed, it can be a fantastic indicator or challenger of honesty, consistency and adequacy. Use the resume checklist to quickly detect potential "lie detector" points, as well as adequate matching with job requirements.

➲ Job applications are great tools for formalizing your pre-screening process. They give you added legal protection and help you avoid the use of illegal personal information sometimes contained in resumes. Never make a hiring decision based solely on a resume; if you have to prove the legality of a decision through the pre-selection process, always refer to job applications, never to resumes.

➲ Use our eight-point "red flag" detector from a job application to determine if an applicant is a potential bad hire and/or a source of potential legal woes.

➲ Online pre-screening automates and speeds up the pre-selection process. It is, more often than not, worthwhile to consider using the pre-screening services of an outside provider. Always use our 6-point checklist to select a pre-screening service company.

➲ Phone screening is your best second level of investigation. Use a standard set of questions to ensure you're evaluating candidates consistently. You may use our suggested short list of questions to ask. Have your phone screening script reviewed by your attorney, as specific State laws may vary.

➲ If you want your company to master the whole hiring process, in compliance with all applicable laws, check our unique workshop, the *No-Fail Hiring System*™ at www.nofailhiring.com.

When it comes to selecting top players, you want to have all four aces of selection in your hands – just keep in mind that no hiring ace is equal.

Chapter

7

The Four Aces of Selection

"Hiring is not about finding people with the right experience. It's about finding people with the right mind-set. Hire for attitude and train for skills."

Peter Carbonara, author of
"Hire for Attitude, Train for Skills" [1]

ALL ACES ARE NOT EQUAL IN HIRING ——————————

This chapter covers the four most important criteria or "aces of selection" you need to apply in interviewing each pre-selected applicant. They are always the same BUT do not weigh equally in the general evaluation of an applicant. In fact, small business owners often allocate the wrong priority of importance to each of them.

These four aces of selection are, in the <u>correct</u> sequence:

- Performance
- Willingness
- Know-how
- Personality

You definitely want to select top players – those who are mostly (1) results-oriented and can naturally perform, (2) willing to work hard and learn, (3) skilled enough to do the job and (4) who ideally also have a great personality. These should be job-related priority criteria.

Yet, when it comes to actually evaluating a candidate's potential, too many business owners and hiring managers let themselves be unconsciously influenced by certain factors (listed in descending degree of importance):

- Personality (good or bad),
- Level of technical skills or "know-how,"
- Willingness to work hard/positive attitude, and
- Ability to perform and demonstrate results.

This unconscious mis-allocation of importance is the most obvious reason of improper candidate selection and the source of most hiring failures. Therefore, we need to re-adjust our mindset and reconfigure the correct sequence in evaluating a candidate.

In each of your interview steps, you need to know what you are looking for and what the correct sequence of evaluation should be.

PERFORMANCE MINDSET:
YOUR ACE OF DIAMONDS

Performance is your primary, most valuable standard of evaluation. The "number one" reason why you hire someone is to get the job done – no matter what it represents. We all agree with that; but how do you then explain that this is usually the most neglected objective criterion used in evaluating pre-selected applicants?

Most business owners and hiring managers evaluate candidates with their heart rather than with their head. Emotions control the process. While everyone agrees that results count first, this criterion is poorly used in selecting new employees. Remember: the worst enemy to hiring is subjectivity (see chapter 4).

A recent study published in *Annals of the New York Academy of Sciences* found that the attractiveness of interviewees can significantly bias outcome in hiring practices. Good-looking applicants (male or female) are usually considered more intelligent and possessing more positive social traits. A recruiter will thus give these pretty boys and girls more chances to get the job, over other, less attractive candidates.[2]

Only results count. If you are looking for results-oriented employees, this is the first, diamond-type check point: is the candidate a <u>natural</u> performer or is he/she mostly an "busy-work" person?

You must be able to differentiate between two opposite types of people: those who are mostly results-oriented and those who are mostly action-oriented. In a small business run by a few people, no one can afford to be just "busy". Whatever your employees are doing, the main purpose of their job is to get things done.

If you had to choose between a mostly results-oriented type of person and a mostly action-oriented one, which one would you pick? It might seem like a simplistic question because the answer is too obvious – at least to you. This does not mean that a high action/energy person has no value: they have value only to the degree that their available energy is effectively used to get results – not just to "do things."

Looking for the performance mindset. Detecting top players who are naturally high performers is your highest priority. There are many "detectors" that you can use in an interview to estimate an applicant's performance mindset. Does the applicant:

- Mention measurable results/achievements in his/her resume or job application?

- Provide references and testimonials which clearly support his/her achievements?

- Provide practical, results-oriented examples of some past performance, rather than mostly action-oriented ones?

- Feel at ease with your results-oriented questions?

- Provide evidence of past performances without any hesitation?

- Communicate in terms of numbers, "dones" or other measurable instances of achievement?

- Respond positively to your on-the-job challenges or simulations and puts his/her attention on solving the situation?

- Go to the point when asked to give own viewpoint on how to handle a difficult job situation?

We are not suggesting that performance mindset is the only criterion; we are saying it is the first one to evaluate. A good reason is that when you put your attention on these "performance mindset" detectors above, the other three aces will appear in a much clearer form.

Example: You are interviewing an applicant for an accountant position. You challenge him on a balance sheet that needs serious prep prior to finalizing the quarterly reports. You focus your evaluation on his ability to come up with some fast solution.

The applicant's attitude and reaction to your challenge enables you to assess his willingness (how he responds to challenges), his level of know-how (his real understanding of balance sheets) and also important soft skills that should be part of his personality (analytical ability, communication, alertness, honesty in his explanation, response to stressful conditions, etc.).

WILLINGNESS: YOUR ACE OF HEARTS _____

Willingness is your second priority in evaluating pre-selected candidates. Many call it "positive attitude." Willingness is a vital soft skill, really. It is part of a person's genuine "personality package." Some people are naturally willing to work hard, to learn more and to do new things. Showing a positive attitude when problems arise can make the difference between hell and paradise on the job and in the working environment, especially when working in a team.

Willingness is a vital attribute because you can't simply force someone to do something if they do not want to. Such persons will do what you want in order to keep their job or to avoid penalties. But they will not really put their heart into it.

With great leadership, you can raise people's willingness. But there are people who do not respond to leadership and who tend to fake willingness. Unfortunately, with such people, you have to apply force and threats in order to get things done.

Why do we allocate a higher priority to willingness, rather than to job-related skills? The reasons are simple and are legally defensible:

- Willingness is a natural attribute but if one does not have it, it can cost you and your company a lot of energy and money.

- You can't buy willingness; one has it or does not. If you think money alone can buy a positive attitude, re-read Chapter 3. Some competitor will soon steal your money-motivated new employees.

- Pre-selected candidates have passed the first job-related skills test. They showed educational and/or professional backgrounds which are compatible with your own job requirements.

- Although a soft skill by nature, willingness is easily proven to be job-related, whatever the job.

- Most importantly, it is hard to teach or improve someone's natural willingness or attitude; whereas you can easily improve most of the needed skills or technical know-how.

DID YOU KNOW?

As reported by Mel Kleiman in *"Hire Tough, Manage Easy,"* the main reason why employees fail is not because they can't do the job but because they won't: [3]

- According to the U.S. Department of Labor, more than 87% of employee failures are due to unwillingness to do the job.

- The Texas Workforce Commission asked 1,000 employers to identify the most important quality an employee should have. Over 85% named positive attitude and willingness to work.

- When asked why they usually fire employees, only 9% of business owners said "inability to do the job." But 69% of them cited attitude-related reasons such as absenteeism and tardiness, bad attitude or work ethics. 22% mentioned other attitude-related reasons.

How to look for willingness. There are a few good detectors that can help you separate top players with high willingness and the right attitude. During your interview session(s), look for the following:

- When asked, the applicant can easily provide examples of situations on the job where he/she had to demonstrate a positive attitude in order to solve a problem or challenge.

- When challenged during a simulation or role playing, the applicant shows evidence of willingness to respond and solve the problems.

- The applicant can show evidence of willingness when he/she had to solve problems in order to help a group.

- Throughout the interview, the applicant shows great willingness in answering your questions and reacts well to your comments on the job challenges and difficulties.

- When checking references, the applicant's willingness and positive attitude comes up as definite qualities.

Have you ever had to work with a very competent but also very unwilling person? You get the idea.

Application. Scott Lowe is Vice President and Chief Information Officer for Westminster College in Fulton, Missouri. An author and regular contributor to *TechRepublic*, he clearly sets the rules about choosing between skills and attitude/willingness in this illustration: [4]

"Candidate #1 has an incredible background and will accept the salary, but his attitude is a little off. Perhaps he feels that IT (Information Technology) is in a 'command and control' role or his ability to work with people is somewhat limited. Candidate #2 has a great attitude and works well with people, but his experience isn't quite up to par with Candidate 1.

"What would you do?

"Here's what I'd do: Dismiss Candidate #1. You can teach hard skills, but teaching attitude or other soft skills is extremely difficult. As for Candidate #2, using a probationary period, I'd likely give that person a chance and see if he can come up to speed in the areas in which he's lacking. Failing that, or if Candidate #2's skill set was simply *too* weak, I'd go back to the well and start the process over."

Lowe had this exact situation when he hired a network administrator. He interviewed a number of people, but the person he ultimately selected wasn't the strongest from a technical perspective. His attitude, however, was really good and his willingness was amazing. Since day one, he worked hard to come up to speed in the necessary areas and has exceeded Scott's expectations, who continually received feedback from people that he'd gone out of his way to professionally handle a task for someone.

Our position is clear. Scott Lowe's opinion best reflects our position: as long as the person satisfies enough of the minimum skills requirements, if he has a good attitude and shows good willingness to make things go right, he's worth his weight in gold. After all, you can teach technical skills... but good luck in teaching willing-ness or positive attitude!

Another positive side of focusing on this second ace is that an applicant will naturally reveal other personality traits or soft skills while exhibiting his/her willingness/positive attitude – or lack thereof.

KNOW-HOW: YOUR ACE OF CLUBS _____

One of the biggest mistakes most employers make when hiring is putting too much emphasis on technical know-how. It is true that many employees get hired for their hard skills and later get fired for their lack of soft ones.

You have already pre-selected applicants on the basis of visible, objective job-based skills and experience. Although this is pushed by the law to be the most important objective criterion for selection, we all know that the most impressive diplomas and technical backgrounds will never guarantee that the job gets done.

All pre-selected applicants have about the same technical (or administra-tive) qualifications; this is why they were pre-selected. But know-how does not mean competency. Most small business employers we work with find it difficult to determine the difference between competencies and know-how (also called hard skills).

In his book *Building Robust Competencies*, Paul Green defines <u>competency</u> as follows: "A written description of measurable work habits and personal skills used to achieve a work objective. They are the underlying characteristics, be-havior, knowledge and skills required to differentiate performance."[5] [6]

Definition. For our purposes, competencies are all the qualities, whether hard skill or soft skill-based, needed to perform a job successfully. Know-how represents only the technical or administrative skills required to perform ex-pertly on a job. These hard skills are usually acquired through education, special training or on-the-job experience. Most of the time, they are the most objec-tive, job-based selection criteria and your most obvious pre-selection criteria.

Examples of hard skills: Hard skills are those tangible and measurable skills that are easy to teach and identify. Some examples of hard skills are occupational skills such as technical and administrative; accounts payable or receivable, financial analysis, typing, machine operation, etc. Hard skills may also include a person's degrees, certifications, position held, and computer expertise.

Evaluation of know-how. The best and easiest way to measure an applicant's practical, non-academic skills, is to put the person to the test. This is your third level of focus during the interview. Here are some important rules, no matter what the desired technical skills are:

- Never trust academic or educational evidence of know-how found in the resume. What was learned at school rarely reflects any ability to actually do the job in your specific work environment.

- Never rely on an applicant's previous experience to demonstrate technical know-how for *your* vacant position. Our golden rule is: know-how can't be measured in the "talking," it can only be measured in the "doing."

- Prior to the interview, create a few situational scenarios you can test an applicant with. Make sure the scenario requires the applicant to demonstrate the required technical skills.

- Test. Do not be afraid: during the interview, put the applicant in a real (best) or simulated (second best) situation and observe his/her actions – and reactions.

Examples of application:

- Give an applicant applying for an accounting job a fictitious balance sheet; allow a few minutes to analyze. Challenge the applicant on the incorrectness of the balance sheet.

- Ask a potential customer service rep to take the phone just for a few minutes; have an employee call and simulate an upset customer. See how the applicant manages the call.

- Ask a computer technician to examine a computer that you "pre-pared" for the interview. See how the applicant handles the problem and manages – or not – to repair the product.

Our position. The most knowledgeable or skilled applicant is not guaranteed to be the most productive employee or even the most motivated one. You are mostly interested in testing hard skills for the purpose of (1) investigating how honest an applicant was in asserting some specific know-how and (2) determining what technical training you need to plan for an applicant to become operational on the job in a short period of time.

DID YOU KNOW?

A national survey of employers, reported in *Inc. Magazine* by Angus Loten, found that high school and college graduates fall short in a number of areas: [7]

- More than 70% of surveyed managers said that recently hired high school students proved to be deficient in basic academic skills, such as grammar, spelling and written communications.

- An overwhelming majority cited problems new hires had handling such routine tasks as writing memos, letters, and other reports. Poor writing skills also proved to be problematic for two-year and four-year college graduates, though to a lesser extent.

- More than 80% of small-business owners reported finding few or no qualified applications, with as many as 12% citing a lack of qualified employees as their biggest business problem.

PERSONALITY: YOUR ACE OF SPADES _____

Why would we consider personality as the last ace of selection, after warning our readers that soft/subjective skills are the most critical attributes to look for, regardless of the job opening? Our explanation is a <u>strategic</u> one:

1. Soft skills – a package of attributes related to personality and behavior, should NOT influence your judgment of the first three selection aces.

2. The first three steps will help you detect those soft skills you decided are job-related and vital for the vacant job.

3. You already have investigated one of the most critical soft skills, which is willingness/attitude.

4. You can't detect a critical soft skill by asking an applicant to exhibit it, but rather by observing the person through the challenges, scenarios and questions asked during the phone screening and interview(s). Hence the sequence.

What is personality, anyway? The word "personality" can be defined as a dynamic and organized set of characteristics possessed by a person that uniquely influences his/her motivations and behaviors in various situations. The word originates from the Latin *persona*, which means mask. Specifically, in the theatre of the ancient Latin-speaking world, the mask was not used as a plot device to *disguise* the identity of a character, but rather was a convention employed to represent or *typify* that character. [8]

Per the above definition, a person may adopt a different personality, depending on the situation or condition he/she is faced with. Under normal circumstances, the person will adopt one personality. In another situation, that same person may be driven to "wear another mask."

Have you ever interviewed a candidate, had a great feeling about the person's attitude and character, yet became very disappointed by his/her personality change, once the "honeymoon" was over? What were you evaluating, really? You were mostly trying to analyze a "mask," or a set of masks, that the applicant would use when going through the interview. He/she might exhibit an entirely different "mask" with other people, once part of the team.

Temporary vs. "chronic" personality. Another challenge is to try to detect an applicant's continuing or chronic personality trait, such as real communication skill, because it is vital for the specific job. The applicant may exhibit such soft skills during the interview. Does it mean that it is a natural, constant quality? The truth is: you don't know. The hard reality is:

- You can't guess if a soft skill or personality characteristic exhibited during an interview is actually constant and natural or just temporary. You need to find out.

- The best way to find out is to put the applicant out of the artificial interview context and "force" him/her to react to real or simulated situations that approximate a real life or business occurrence. It is well known that people reveal themselves best when confronted by un- anticipated situations. This is what corporate and professional hiring managers call "competency-based interviews."

Why is personality your Ace of Spades? If you play cards, you might know that the Ace of Spades usually has the highest rank (such as in bridge and poker) but it can, at times, be the lowest. It is usually called the death card and is also a symbol of war.

Personality can be called your hiring "death card" for two good reasons. First, if you allow yourself to be influenced by an applicant's temporary personality, chances are you will fail and hire the wrong people. You would never hire someone wearing a mask, would you?

Second, you definitely need to detect those vital job-related soft skills because you know this is what will determine success on the job. So the key question is: how do you avoid hiring people wearing masks?

How to detect vital soft skills. Our experience has shown that the simplest and most effective approach in detecting job-related personality factors is the following:

DID YOU KNOW?

In a three-year study conducted by *Leadership IQ,* a leadership training company from Washington D.C., 5,247 hiring managers from 312 public, private, business and healthcare organizations were examined. Collectively, these managers hired more than 20,000 employees during the study period. [9]

The study focused on why new hires fail at such alarming rates which is certainly a growing trend:

- 46% of newly-hired employees will fail within 18 months, while only 19% will achieve unequivocal success.

- Contrary to popular belief, technical skills are not the first reason why new hires fail. Instead, poor interpersonal skills dominate the list:
    - 26% of new hires fail because they can't accept feedback.
    - 23% of new hires fail because they're unable to understand and manage emotions.
    - 17% of new hires fail because they lack the necessary motivation to excel.
    - 15% of new hires fail because they have the wrong temperament for the job.
    - Only 11% of new hires failed because they lack the necessary technical skills.
- During the study, 812 managers experienced significantly more hiring success than their peers. What differentiated their interviewing approach was their emphasis on interpersonal and motivational issues.

Per Mark Murphy, CEO of Leadership IQ, hiring failures can be prevented if managers focus most of their interviewing energy on candidates' coachability, emotional intelligence, motivation and temperament.

1) When you develop your job description, make a list of soft skills vital to the job. Describe, in writing, why each of these soft skills is important. This gives you better legal protection.

2) Honesty being a crucial soft skill, you can start checking it through resumes/job applications and phone screenings. If you have doubts or reservations, challenge the applicant on any nebulous topic during the interview. Also use reference and background checks to confirm your doubts.

3) During the first interview, focus on the first three Aces. Ensure that you have prepared simulations or scenarios that challenge the applicant on each of these selection criteria. Remember: people reveal themselves best when they are confronted with unprepared or unexpected situations. Challenge is the key word.

4) Take note of the applicant's reactions to each of your questions and challenges. See next chapter for questions to ask – or not.

5) You can now ask the applicant to demonstrate that he/she does have the required soft skills. You do so by suggesting that he/she explains how a specific soft skill was used in order to solve a problem or to respond to a challenge. See chapter 4.

What are the most important soft skills? No matter what the job is, you should always check for some crucial soft skills. Based on our experience and many studies, the following are absolutely basic to every job and in any working environment. Chapters 8 and 9 address interview techniques and provide practical tips for detecting these. We advise that you systematically:

–   Include these crucial soft skills in the job description and

–   Attach the following table (or equivalent) to your interview procedure and complete it for each applicant.

Final note on justifying your job-related soft skills. You should, whenever possible, justify every required soft skill for a specific job. The table below represents only what we consider the basic soft skills applicable, whatever the job. However, we advise that you personalize their justification for each specific position. Visit www.nofailhiring.com to access a sample of soft skills justification text.

TABLE OF BASIC SOFT SKILLS

Date:_____   Applicant's name: _____

Position: _____	High	Medium	Low	Don't know
◆ Honesty	____	____	____	____
◆ Willingness (a)	____	____	____	____
◆ Creativity (b)	____	____	____	____
◆ Manageability (c)	____	____	____	____
◆ Temperament (d)	____	____	____	____
◆ Challenge-driven	____	____	____	____
◆ Drive/self-motivation	____	____	____	____
◆ Communication skills	____	____	____	____
◆ Tolerance to pressure	____	____	____	____
◆ Analytical capacities	____	____	____	____

Notes:

(a) Eager to work hard, to learn and to do new things. It is also about positive attitude. This is your Ace of Diamonds.

(b) Ability to create or contribute to new ideas and to innovate. Includes ability to find solutions to problems.

(c) Ability to accept and implement orders or feedback from bosses, colleagues, customers and others.

(d) General attitude towards others, including teamwork. Also called inter-relationship skills.

DID YOU KNOW?

WORKING WITH "GENERATION Y"

Born between 1980 and 2000, the Millennials – also called Generation Y, GenNext, the Google Generation or even the Tech Generation – are 76 million strong and compose the fastest-growing segment of workers today. Unlike the Gen-Xers and the Boomers, they have developed work characteristics and tendencies from doting parents, structured lives and contact with diverse people. Millennials are used to working in teams and want to make friends with people at work. Millennials work well with diverse co-workers.

Millennials also make their "older" peers quite worried about their very different work ethic, lack of loyalty, over-confidence and self-esteem, lack of respect for hierarchy and an exaggerated entitlement attitude. As Lynne C. Lancaster and David Stillman describe it so well in their new book *"The M-Factor"*:

> *"A generation gap is at its saddest. However people phrase it, everyone seems to agree that Millennials are the entitled generation… It's become a real source of resentment in the workplace."*[10]

Lancaster and Stillman recommend that employers and recruiters learn to know and understand Millennials better. They warn against some hiring procedure mistakes that make them run away from a job opening and also provide smart advice for keeping them happy and motivated on the job.

We strongly recommend *"The M-Factor"* if you are concerned about increasing your workforce with Millennials in the years to come. Per the book's authors, this generation is still increasing and will likely surpass the 80-million-member baby boomer generation in size, in the 2010 Census.

Hence, a good reason to know them better…

NO-FAIL HIRING TIPS

- ● Use the four aces of selection to systematically evaluate each applicant: performance mindset, willingness, know-how and personality. Like playing cards, these Aces are your most important "hiring cards," yet they are not equal in value. You must know exactly what you want to measure and in which sequence.

- ● **Performance mindset: Your Ace of Diamonds.** Detecting top players who are naturally high performers is your highest priority. Use the suggested "detectors" in the interview to estimate if an applicant has a strong performance mindset – or not.

- ● **Willingness: Your Ace of Hearts.** To a large degree you can improve technical skills; but how do you improve attitude? Never compromise with this vital fact: people get hired for their hard skills and get fired for their lack of soft ones. A positive attitude is such a vital soft skill that you want to measure it as soon as you can in the hiring process.

- ● **Know-how: Your Ace of Clubs.** You want to have competent employees who can at least master the basic technical skills as required on the job. The golden rule is: never trust what they say, always test what they should be able to do. Know-how is measured in the doing, not in the talking.

- ● **Personality: Your Ace of Spades.** We measure personality last; not because it is the least important evaluation criterion but because if you let yourself be influenced by a "nice" personality, it could offer trouble, or even, potentially, destroy your business! The golden rule is: never trust what you see, because you don't know if it is real!

- ● Detecting if an applicant possesses the right hard and soft skills in less than one hour is hardly an exact science. But you can maximize the objectivity of your evaluation with the *No-Fail Hiring System*™. Visit www.nofailhiring.com to find out how you can double or even triple the effectiveness of your hiring procedure.

Interviewing a candidate is often like learning how to manage on a blind date. Both usually end up with the desperate hope that you are making a smart move!

Chapter

8

Your First Interview Scenario

"What is a date, really, but a job interview that lasts all night? The only difference between a date and a job interview is that in not many job interviews is there a chance you'll end up naked at the end of it."

Jerry Seinfeld,
Stand-up comedian,
writer and actor. [1]

A TWO-STEP INTERVIEW STRATEGY _____

Proceeding systematically with two interviews minimum – not just one — is your best bet in dramatically raising the objectivity of your judgment...and minimizing the odds of regretting your hiring decision.

Why not just conduct one interview? Conducting one long interview with a qualified applicant will always leave you with doubts, false impressions and potentially painful regrets. If, for whatever reason, you feel that you want to hire an applicant "right away" after that first interview, ask yourself the following questions:

– Do I have enough data to make a rational, non-emotional hiring decision?

– Did I collect enough evidence about past performance?

– Do I have optimal certainty about the applicant's honesty, loyalty, willingness and other critical soft skills?

– Do I have enough data from background checks or criminal records that would minimize the odds of legal trouble?

If your company does not have an established Human Resource Department, our recommendation is as follows: ask a trusted assistant to conduct the phone screening/interview. Then the first interview can be conducted by that same person and by the person who will manage the new employee. The second interview should be done by that same manager AND the business owner if a decision is to be made at the end of that interview. You can also decide to conduct a third one yourself if the vacant job is critical for the company.

Being involved as the business owner, even if only in the last step of the hiring mission, is important for two reasons: (1) people want to know who they are working for and, ultimately, they all work for you; and (2) you want to exercise a senior quality control on the recruitment procedure – using the proper evaluation criteria. After all, the business owner is the one who should closely supervise the most important decisions for the company's future.

First interview format. Pre-selected applicants who pass the phone screening test should be invited to visit your company for a first interview. Its purposes, in order of importance, are:

1. <u>Follow up on pre-screening</u>. Clarify with the applicant any point left unclear from the pre-screening step.

2. <u>Past performance</u>. Question the applicant about any asserted past achievements – whether on a job or in life.

3. <u>Future performance</u>. Determine the applicant's potential ability to perform on the job, in your working environment. This can only be done through a series of job-related questions, challenges or simulations.

4. <u>Willingness</u>. This vital soft skill can be evaluated throughout the first interview. Make sure whoever conducts it has full attention on it while asking the various questions and presenting challenges to the applicant.

5. <u>Know-how</u>. Does the applicant have the basic hard skills to operate on the job? This is determined through simulations and challenges, not through conversation.

6. <u>Personality/soft skills</u>. Does the applicant have the necessary job-related soft skills? Keep the soft skills checklist at hand and complete it right after the interview.

7. <u>Motivation and intentions</u>. What motivates the applicant to find a job and to work? The fact that this is only the 7th criterion does not mean it is not important. But after going through the first 6 steps, applicants will have a hard time lying about their true motivations.

8. <u>Your own impression</u>. At the conclusion of this first interview, the recruiter must be able to answer the simple question: "Would I want to work with this person?" This decision should evolve naturally from going through the 7 previous steps. It also dictates if the applicant should be invited back for a second interview.

THE REACTIONAL JOB INTERVIEWING™ TECHNIQUE _____

Not just behavioral. The interview method we teach is called *Reactional Job Interviewing™*: it "forces" applicants to react naturally to a prepared scenario. It leads them to be "themselves," rather than acting artificially in order to "pass the test."

Reactional job interviewing is more effective than typical behavioral-type interviews, as widely used in the corporate world. These techniques, also called situational or competency-based interviews, consist of asking the candidate to provide specific examples of past achievements and/or behaviors that demonstrate a required competency or behavior relevant to the specific job vacancy. The theory is that the best way to predict future performance is to examine an applicant's past and present performance in a similar situation.

Our *No-Fail Hiring™* System goes one vital step further than just asking questions about past performance and behavior. It challenges applicants, provokes them and "forces" them to reveal their true nature. Remember: only through unexpected circumstances will most people reveal their true hard and, most importantly, soft skills.

It is all about reactions. What is more important than the answer to the question asked? <u>It's the reaction to the question</u>! Always observe an applicant's immediate reaction to your question or challenge. Doing so will tell you more than just the answer. Someone may give you a perfect answer to a question, while perfectly lying. You can't really detect a chronic, constant personality in an answer – because the applicant may know the perfect answer to the question.

Example. You ask: "What were you doing between [period] and [period]? – knowing that the applicant's job application contains holes in his job history. The applicant gives you a logical answer. But he stumbles in his explanation and takes a while to get the answer. You then challenge him to provide a name for reference check purposes. He starts to get nervous and loses his temper, showing his real personality — and his intention to hide something.

We will see more examples in the next pages.

Rules on conducting a reactional job interview. In order to minimize subjectivity and maximize certainty in your evaluation, make sure that you follow these simple but extremely important rules:

1. **Standard interview format**. Create an interview report form which includes all job-related questions to be asked, challenges or simulations to be presented, along with a standard evaluation and rating system. Applicants must be interviewed using the same rating system, no matter who is conducting the interview.

2. **Preparedness**. Ensure that you have all standard pre-screening and interview documents ready in the applicant's folder. Never start an interview without them. Each applicant should read the job description prior to the interview.

3. **Control**. You must control the interview. This means that you should focus on asking questions, presenting challenges and getting the answers; this is the way to get to know applicants. Make them talk and (re)act.

4. **Job-related questions only**. Always ask the same job-related questions to applicants. If you ask a non-standard question, write it down and explain why you asked it. Remember, standard procedure is your best legal protection. You must be able to prove and document the job-relatedness for each question asked. See examples in the next pages.

5. **Job-related challenges and simulations**. Make sure you always use the same job-related challenge or simulation scenario for all pre-selected applicants. Questions are not enough; challenge applicant's answers in case of doubt or if you're not convinced. See examples in the next pages.

6. **Observe and listen**. You can't learn about an applicant if you do all the talking. Put your attention on observing how the applicant reacts to your questions and challenges. Do not guide his/her answers or help with an answer.

7. **Ideal answers**. You must know the ideal answer to each of your ques-

tions and scenarios. We advise that you write down such ideal answers prior to an interview, as part of your hiring procedure. Doing so will minimize the subjectivity (and legal liability) related to your evaluation.

8. **Timing.** Apply discipline to your interview schedule. Even if an applicant seems extremely qualified, make sure to clearly separate the first and the second interviews. Stick to your standard first interview format as much as possible.

9. **Interview report**. Use a standard report form with uniform evaluation and measurement criteria. Do not deviate from that report format. Take job-related notes of applicants' answers AND reactions to your questions or challenges. Do not invite trouble by writing personal notes on applications and report forms which could be viewed as discriminatory in a legal action.

10. **Train on the procedure**. Ensure every person involved in the hiring process is trained and drilled on the whole hiring procedure and interview technique. A good way to practice is to have one person conduct the actual interview while another takes notes and fills out the interview report form. But it starts with training. And it offers additional legal protection.

THE RIGHT & WRONG QUESTIONS TO ASK

Illegal questions. First of all, let us look at the questions you should <u>never</u> ask, as you would risk huge legal liabilities. The EEOC has determined several types of questions to be discriminatory. Among these are the following:

- Questions which discriminate on the basis of gender, religion, race/color or national origin. In order to avoid potential claims of discrimination in violation of Title VII of the Civil Right Act, you should avoid the following or similar questions:

- What is your religion?

- What church do you attend?

- Are you married?

- Are you a national citizen? If not, where do you come from?

- Do you have or do you plan to have children?

- What is your maiden name?

- Questions which discriminate on the basis of some disabilities. The Americans with Disabilities Act of 1990 prohibits employment dis-

DID YOU KNOW?

YOUR PERSONAL INTERVIEW NOTES COULD COST YOU A LOT OF TROUBLE.

In the *Modtland v. Mills Fleet Farm Inc.* case (No. Civ.04-3051, D. Minn., 2004), a group of applicants sued a farming-supply company for discrimination based on sex and race. The company had given applicants written tests and the hiring manager had noted the applicants' race and sex on the test. Its well-meaning goal: to assess whether the test had a disparate impact on minority hiring.

The plaintiffs argued that the practice amounted to an illegal, pre-offer inquiry. The company responded that it merely "observed" the applicants' race and sex and didn't require applicants to disclose the information.

A district court disagreed. While the company didn't formally request the data, it still technically required the information for employment. As a result, the court let the applicant group pursue a class-action suit. [2]

Solution:

Do not add personal notes to a standard application form. Write any personal note on a separate paper and do not add it to the applicant's folder.

crimination against qualified applicants as well as employees. Avoid the following or similar questions:

– Do you have any disability that could prevent you from doing this specific job?

– Could your disability interfere with your effectiveness?

– Do you have a [specific] condition or disease?

• The Age Discrimination in Employment Act of 1967 prohibits age discrimination in employment against individuals who are 40 years of age or older. Avoid questions like these:

– How old are you?

– When did you graduate (or finish school)?

– What is your date of birth?

In addition to these federal employment discrimination laws, your company may also be subject to state employment discrimination laws. Check with an employment attorney or your state employment department of labor to determine whether your business is complying with state employment discrimination laws.

Other "dangerous" questions. Most business owners know the obvious illegal questions they can't ask job applicants. But sometimes, the most seemingly innocuous exchanges can put you in peril of violating discrimination laws. Here are some other fringe areas to avoid:

– "Do you belong to any clubs or social organizations?" You may want to know about workers' hobbies or extracurricular activities, but this question can reveal info about workers' political or religious affiliations, which are not job-related.

– "Where do you live?" You cannot pick applicants based on where they live, for the obvious reasons: some neighborhoods are heavily populated by certain ethnic groups.

– "How many sick days did you take last year?" This question could be interpreted as digging into a candidate's personal health information – and that is legally prohibited.

– "What does your wife do for a living?" This is an invasion of privacy; you are not even supposed to know or inquire if the applicant is married.

What questions can you ask, then? To fully comply with the applicable federal and state laws, you must be able to prove that your questions are job-related and/or directly pertaining to your industry and are not interfering with the applicant's right to privacy. If you have any concern about an applicant's qualification because of some personal characteristics or attributes, ensure that you justify the job relatedness of your question(s). Some examples:

– Instead of asking "Are you a U.S. citizen?" ask: "We need to ensure that we hire people who are legally authorized to work in the country; can you provide evidence you have authorization to work in the U.S.?"

– Instead of asking "Could your family responsibilities prevent you from working overtime?" ask: "This job requires travelling and overtime work, as we do trade shows and fairs; can you accommodate such an overtime schedule on a regular basis?"

– If you need someone who can endure physical stress on the job, such as carrying heavy loads, do not ask if the applicant is in good shape; rather, ask: "This job requires being able to carry heavy packages – sometimes over 50 pounds; it puts serious stress on the body. Can you perform such task every day – understanding that it is part of the job description?"

– If you need someone who has no serious criminal record for a high-trust position, do not ask if the applicant was ever arrested. Rather, ask "This job is a high-trust position as it requires constant contact with our privileged customers. Are there any crime convictions we should know about?"

– If you suspect that an applicant is too young for a specific job, avoid asking how old he/she is. Rather, you can ask "As the job description specifies, this job requires the employee to be older than 18. Do you meet this requirement?"

- Do not ask: "Can you sit for long periods?" but "As this job requires constant phone communication with customers, is there any reason why you could not handle phone contact every day, at a desk?"

- Instead of asking: "Are you a member of some association or group?" ask: "Are you a member of any group relevant to our industry?"

- Instead of asking: "How far from the office do you live?" ask: "Are you able to start work at 9 a.m.?" You just want to know if the person can get to work during your operating hours.

- Don't ask: "How many sick days did you take last year?" Rather, ask: "How many days of work did you miss last year?

- Don't ask applicant: "Do you have a problem working with a male (female) boss?" – You would rather ask: "This job is supervised by a male (female) manager. What is your experience with male (female) managers or supervisors?

POWERFUL REACTIONAL-TYPE INTERVIEW QUESTIONS

As stated earlier, these questions not only investigate an applicant's past achievements and/or behaviors; they also force them to react naturally and instantly. This reactional approach needs to be supported by challenge and simulation scenarios.

Remember: the reaction to a question can be more important than the answer itself. The following are some examples of different questions and scenarios which follow the first interview format, as presented at the beginning of this chapter. Examples:

- *Pre-screening adequacy (if you need to clarify any nebulous point from the job application)*

  - **Question**: "What were you doing between [period] and [period}? Answer: "I took 2 years off for personal reasons." After the applicant has answered:

  - **Challenge**: "Can you mention something you achieved during that period which could prove beneficial for this job opening?" Then:

  - **Challenge**: "Could anyone confirm or attest to such achievement?"

- *Performance mindset (is the applicant more results-oriented than mostly action-oriented?)*

  - **Question**: "Your application form mentions (____) years of experience as a sales representative. What results did you get on that job? Answer: "I reached my sales target every single year." Then:

  - **Challenge**: "Who could confirm that?" Or: "How can we verify that?"

  - **Question**: "Can you tell us of some past achievements which would impress us?" When the applicant answers:

  - **Challenge**: "Thank you. How could such an achievement benefit your activities on this specific job?"

  - **Question**: "Tell us about a difficult problem you had to face and resolve at work." When the applicant answers:

  - **Challenge**: "What was the solution? How did you develop that solution? What was the outcome? What would your management say about it if we asked?"

  - **Question**: "Tell us about a mistake you made at work. How did you handle it?" when the applicant answers:

  - **Challenge**: "Demonstrate how you handled this mistake to prevent it from occurring again. Explain what measures you took and how your management or colleagues reacted. What was the end result?"

- *Willingness/attitude (can also be measured during challenges on hard skill simulations)*

  - **Simulation**: "We need evidence of some important technical skills on this job, as well as a strong problem-solving mindset for unexpected technical problems, while servicing customers. Can you please have a look at this computer and let us know, in about 10 minutes, what the problem is – and what you suggest to rectify the problem(s)."

  - **Question**: "Say you get a phone call from a very upset customer. As the customer service department supervisor, how are you going to handle it?"

  - **Challenge/Simulation**: "Can you please answer the phone, there is an upset customer waiting to be helped ..."

  - **Question**: "Describe a time when you had to demonstrate your coping skills, during some previous stressful job situation?" When the applicant answers:

  - **Challenge/Simulation**: "There is currently some elevated stress and tension in the department where the job opening is. Explain how you would manage to be accepted and to help reduce group stress."

- *Measurement of specific job-related soft skills (detecting personality traits and behaviors that are vital for the job).*

  - **Question**: "Tell us of a time you had to demonstrate good communication skills to handle a conflict situation." When the applicant answers:

  - **Challenge**: "How would others attest to such skill?"

  - **Challenge**: "Your job application indicates that you have changed jobs 4 times in the last 3 years. How do you explain that?" When the applicant answers:

- **Challenge**: "We are concerned that this may represent a lack of stability – knowing that it is a key criterion for success on this job opening. How can you prove otherwise?"

- **Question**: "Can you tell us about a specific contribution to a group that demonstrated good team spirit?" When the applicant answers:

- **Challenge**: "Who could attest to that?"

- **Question**: "This job requires strong time management capabilities. Please describe an experience which could lead us to think you have what it takes regarding your ability to multi-task as well as being effective in a high-stress working environment."

IMPORTANT NOTES

- As an interviewer, learn to observe the applicant's reactions to your questions and challenges. Listening is silver but observing is gold, as it allows you to SEE how the applicant reacts.

- Develop your first interview questions and scenarios for a specific job prior to starting your hiring mission for that job. Do not deviate from your scenario – or deviate as little as possible.

- If you are afraid of challenging a candidate, ask yourself that question: do you want to wait until you regret that you did not do it? The good news is: top players will love your challenges. Others will run away... which is what we call "natural selection."

THE 8 MOST LETHAL FIRST INTERVIEW BLUNDERS

1. **Failure to prepare for and/or follow the first interview format**. If you start an interview with no formalized questions and no knowledge of what you are looking for, you're opening the door to trouble.

2. **Failure to focus**. You want to measure if the applicant possesses the necessary job-related hard and soft skills. Any other issue is unnecessary or should be left to the second interview.

3. **Ignoring the 4 aces of selection.** Many business owners and their hiring managers focus too much on personality and forget the higher importance of other aces.

4. **Talking too much.** You need to focus on (1) observing and (2) listening. The more an applicant reacts and talks, the more you are able to discover about his/her hard and soft skills.

5. **Being afraid of asking tough questions.** Remember: only soft players will either resist or avoid your questions. Do not fall in the sympathy trap because you think one applicant is nice. Being effective has sometimes nothing to do with "being nice."

6. **Falling in the "halo effect" trap.** Most people naturally tend to stick to their first impressions. We also tend to perceive others as we are. Avoid the emotion trap!

7. **Helping applicants.** Do not ask leading questions to help an applicant "pass the test." Do not answer the questions for them. Don't be afraid to wait for the applicant to answer.

8. **Invading privacy.** Enough has been said about that. Trying to find out about privacy-related issues on an applicant only leads to potential legal trouble.

A FINAL NOTE:

It takes a lot of training and practice to effectively conduct hiring interviews. This is often the reason for lack of interest or blind desire to delegate this vital function. Think about it this way: would you delegate the first interview with a future marital partner?

NO-FAIL HIRING TIPS

⊃ Never limit your hiring procedure to one single interview. There are too many variables to be analyzed before you have optimal certainty about an applicant's potential. The second interview has a totally different purpose but can't be done effectively if you fail to follow the golden rules in the first one.

⊃ Stick to your first interview format for ALL applicants. Do not deviate from your chosen format, as it could lead to potential legal trouble in the event an applicant files a discrimination complaint. All applicants must be treated equally.

⊃ Practice our unique *Reactional Job Interviewing™* technique. It "forces" applicants to react naturally, from a prepared scenario. It leads them to be natural or more "themselves," rather than acting artificially in order to "pass the test."

⊃ Prepare your challenging questions and simulations prior to conducting a first hiring interview. Never start an interview without being prepared for a specific vacant position.

⊃ Learn to observe first and listen second. Do not help an applicant answer the questions, as your most important evaluation criterion is often the reaction to a question – rather than just the answer.

⊃ If you need help in establishing an effective, standard hiring procedure in your company, visit www.nofailhiring.com. We specialize in training business owners and their trusted executives or assistants on the reactional interviewing technique. We also help you establish a standard hiring department, complete with all technical and legal forms.

The *No-Fail Hiring System™* guarantees to double, even triple the effectiveness of your hiring procedure. The rate of success approaches 90% if all tools and techniques are applied correctly.

Part C

The Decision
Process

Preparing for the second interview is very much like a forensic investigation; you use tests and techniques on applicants to assess the probability of trouble or success.

Chapter

9

Prelude to The Second Interview

"Recruiting is hard. It's just finding the needles in the haystack. We do it ourselves and we spend a lot of time at it. I've participated in the hiring of maybe 5,000-plus people in my life. So I take it very seriously. You can't know enough in a one-hour interview."

Steve Jobs,
Founder of *Apple.* [1]

FOLLOWING UP ON THE
FIRST INTERVIEW

There are three actions to undertake before you meet a selected applicant again. These actions are crucial to the quality of your decision. They can double or even triple the quality of your evaluation. Not going through these steps systematically may cost you trouble or a hire.

First interview general evaluation. Your first step is to formally summarize and score your first interview impressions. Determine what attributes you were able to clearly detect, related to both the applicant's hard and soft skills. You also need to question and focus on those attributes you were NOT able to detect that are important for optimal job effectiveness.

At the end of the first interview, spend a couple of minutes completing your applicant report form. Remember, this form needs to be used uniformly for every interviewed applicant. Use the first interview format to score each applicant, right after the interview. It could look like this:

FIRST INTERVIEW SUMMARY EVALUATION TABLE

NAME:_____   Date: _____   Position: _____

		Excellent	Good	Fair	Poor
1)	Phone pre-screening	____	____	____	____
2)	Past performance/track record	____	____	____	____
3)	Future performance potential	____	____	____	____
4)	Willingness	____	____	____	____
5)	Know-how	____	____	____	____
6)	Personality/soft skills	____	____	____	____
7)	Motivation/intentions	____	____	____	____
8)	Own impression at end	____	____	____	____

NOTES:

(Write down job-related-only notes that can support your own impression above.)

You should also fill out a soft skills table, as given below. There might be more soft skills required for a specific position. We advise that you work at measuring a maximum number of soft skills, even if some of them are not considered vital for the specific job. The reason is simple: you want to face the fact that there are certain things you do NOT know about an applicant.

Below is an example of an extended soft skills table, the first 10 usually being the most important ones, whatever the job is:

SOFT SKILLS EVALUATION TABLE

Date: _____   Applicant's name: _____

Position:_____	High	Medium	Low	Don't know
Honesty	____	____	____	____
Willingness	____	____	____	____
Creativity	____	____	____	____
Manageability	____	____	____	____
Temperament	____	____	____	____
Challenge-driven	____	____	____	____
Drive/self-motivation	____	____	____	____
Communication skills	____	____	____	____
Tolerance to pressure	____	____	____	____
Analytical capacities	____	____	____	____
Loyalty	____	____	____	____
Enthusiasm	____	____	____	____
Presentation	____	____	____	____
Dynamism	____	____	____	____
Listening skills	____	____	____	____
Persuasion skills	____	____	____	____
Tolerance	____	____	____	____
Administrative skills	____	____	____	____
Ambition	____	____	____	____

Important note:

Complete the previous table, no matter how confident you might or might not be, regarding the scoring of a specific trait after the first interview. Why? Because it forces you to recognize that you don't know something about that applicant. This is the exact reason for going through such a procedure.

Once you have gone through this personal "quality control," you can then decide to continue the hiring procedure with the next two steps, PRIOR TO conducting a second interview.

PRE-EMPLOYMENT TESTS: USE THEM WISELY

The legality challenge. Many pre-employment tests exist on the market. More than 3,000 firms offer pre-employment testing services to assess technical or administrative ability, personality and medical conditions. Good tests can reveal skills and capabilities that you might not glean from an application or an interview. Such tests can also lower the incidence of theft and accidents in the workplace and reduce the likelihood of negligent-hiring suits.

If you decide to test applicants, you must ensure that the tests you use (1) don't discriminate, (2) are required of all candidates without exception and (3) assess skills or aptitudes relevant to the position being filled. In other words, any assessment used must be strictly job-related.

Is pre-employment testing legal? The answer is "Yes, but." The "yes" answer qualifies as long as a pre-employment test is administered according to the test developer's intended use. It isn't the test that is "legal" or "illegal," it is the APPLICATION of the test that makes the difference! Simply stated, if you use a test to measure specific attributes that are needed on the job, it must exhibit evidence of validity in evaluating such attributes. Additionally, such tests would have to be administered to every candidate for the same position without exception. Proceeding differently would open the door to legal trouble.

For example, you could administer an accounting aptitude test to all candidates for an accountant position. But administering such test only to a few candidates for that position would be discriminatory. Doing so would definitely be considered a discriminatory practice by the EEOC and would expose you to legal issues.

In recent years there has been a lot of misinformation published regarding the legality of using pre-employment assessments. One question often asked is: does the EEOC or the Office of Federal Contract Compliance validate pre-employment assessments? The answer is definitely no. The extent of their authority is to audit or investigate unacceptable procedures when a discrimination charge has resulted from adverse impact. Their investigation does not just target pre-employment tests but pertains to all employee selection procedures.

Your most serious concern is to stay away from tests that have been shown to have a "disproportionate adverse impact" on minorities, women and the physically challenged, unless you can demonstrate a business necessity for them. This issue is strictly regulated by the Federal Government's *Uniform Guidelines on Employee Selection Procedures* (see chapter 2).

You may obtain a copy of the *Uniform Guidelines* from the U.S. Government Printing Office by calling (888) 293-6498 or on the Web at www.gpo.gov.

When should you administer tests? The best time to suggest a candidate to complete a test is after the first interview. Three reasons for this: (1) you have already pre-selected the applicant on observable, objective criteria, so the test results should not entirely challenge your observations; (2) the applicant has been introduced to your company and feels more at ease with your hiring procedure; and (3) every pre-selected applicant will be more willing to go through the testing process if they know they are of potential interest to you.

We strongly recommend that you do NOT use any pre-employment test prior to meeting an applicant for the first interview. Our philosophy is that any assessment should either comfort your first evaluation or challenge some specific attributes which you observed to be lacking or weakly measured during the interview. But no test by itself should ever lead you to make a decision to hire – or not to hire.

Whenever you consider using any pre-employment test, ensure that the test provider can issue evidence of non-adverse impact as well as validity and job-relatedness. Remember that the main cause of complaints to the EEOC stem from invasion of privacy, discrimination against minorities and irrelevance to the job.

What tests can be used as pre-employment supports? There are various tests which can be used to help assess a pre-selected applicant. Here are just a few examples:

<u>Achievement or skill tests</u> verify an applicant's specific skill in performing a job. For example, a secretary could be tested on how many words he/she can type per minute. A candidate for an accountant position could be asked to perform an accounting test. An applicant for a financial manager position could perform a general finance test.

<u>Physical tests</u> assess a candidate's strength, coordination and other physical attributes. Warning: these tests can be viewed as keeping women or people older than 40 from being hired for physically demanding jobs. To avoid discrimination charges, ensure that tests are administered to male and female applicants of all ages and are solely related to the job's essential functions. Note that per the American Disabilities Act (ADA), you may be required to assist a disabled applicant in meeting the physical demands of the job.

Also keep in mind that for individuals with disabilities, the ADA has created the right to be free from pre-offer medical examinations in the hiring process. Specifically, the Act provides that "*a covered entity shall not conduct a medical examination or make inquiries of a job applicant as to whether such applicant is an individual with a disability or as to the nature or severity of such disability.*"[2]

However, an employer may make pre-employment inquiries into the ability of an applicant to perform job-related functions and may also "*require a medical examination after an offer of employment has been made to a job applicant, and prior to the commencement of the employment duties of such applicant, and may condition an offer of employment on the results of such examination*"[3] so long as: 1) *'all entering employees are subjected to such an examination regardless of disability' [4]; 2) the 'information obtained regarding the medical condition or history of the applicant' is kept confidential,[5] and 3) the 'examination is shown to be job-related and consistent with business necessity.' [6]*

Aptitude tests measure one's general knowledge and learning potential. They can evaluate verbal aptitude, numerical skills, space perception, form recognition, clerical ability, motor coordination, finger dexterity and manual adroitness. Make sure that ALL the questions on the test are applicable to the job for which you are considering hiring an applicant. Do not base a hiring decision on the results of any non-applicable question(s).

We also recommend that you double check any Intelligent Quotient (IQ) test that you plan to use. Many IQ tests fail to demonstrate a person's real ability to solve problems. Challenges and simulations during interviews are often better predictors.

Drug tests are not considered medical examinations under the Americans with Disabilities Act, so they may be given before offering someone a job. However, the ADA prohibits alcohol testing until after you have made a conditional job offer. To find out what types of testing your state allows and their special requirements, check with your state's labor department. Then prepare a written drug testing policy.

Inform all applicants and employees of your drug testing policy and always obtain a signed and dated consent form before you administer any drug test. If you ask candidates to take a drug test as a condition of employment, issue fair warning to them on your job application form. Check with your attorney and consult state laws where the covered employees work.

Personality tests are the most popular assessment tools used by companies today to detect job-related soft skills. An estimated 40% of Fortune 100 companies include some form of psychological testing in their employment selection systems. A similar survey by the American Management Association showed that 44% of its responding members used testing to select employees.[9]

Employers use different types of personality tests for different purposes. For example, a product sales company might use a measure of aggressiveness to

DID YOU KNOW?

**TESTING JOB APLICANTS IS WORTH
MORE THAN THE LEGAL RISK**

Many small businesses tend to shy away from pre-employment testing, under the advice of their attorneys. The main argument is that organizations that have used tests have been sued.

But per Ira S. Wolfe, founder of *Success Performance Solutions* and author of *Perfect Labor Storm 2.0* [7], it is also true that more businesses have been sued because they *didn't* use testing. Every hiring decision carries a risk. But you need to know the facts:

- In 2007, the EEOC heard 77,000 discrimination complaints.

- Of those 77,000, only 304 involved pre-employment assessments.

- Of those 304 complaints related to assessments, the decisions that ruled in favor of the employee were related to the improper use of the assessment, not to the validity of the assessment itself.

Says Wolfe: "As long as the test is valid, reliable, non-discriminatory AND job-related, the use of pre-employment tests is a best practice that meets EEOC guidelines. If your attorney can't substantiate why he/she believes pre-employment tests should be avoided with anything more than it's his/her opinion, get a second opinion." [8]

select applicants for a sales job so that their characteristics match successful incumbents in their sales force. Perhaps the most commonly used personality tests are honesty or integrity tests. Integrity tests are designed to predict proclivity to theft and other forms of counterproductive work behavior in job applicants.

Our position about pre-employment tests. Used intelligently, good tests can provide valuable information, specifically about issues that were difficult to detect during interviews. We recommend the following dispositions in the use of any test:

a. Make sure that the suggested assessment has been validated by the provider and does not discriminate applicants based on race, gender, ethnicity or other background factor.

b. Verify that the test was developed for job-related-only applications. Avoid tests which investigate private matters and other non-professional issues.

c. Tests are not the "ultimate weapon." They can potentially increase the quality of hiring, assuming you make testing part of a well-designed and well-managed hiring process.

d. Measure the results. Test the test on your best employees. This will give you a better understanding of how a specific test functions and its limits.

e. In doubt, trust your guts. Always question unexpected test results and take it up with the applicant. Most applicants will have something to say about bad results, which is often the most interesting part of testing.

f. Tests can be faked. Some applicants do not hesitate to find out about specific popular tests and will even train to pass them. The best test is to have someone in your company "test the test." If it does not pass that test, do not use it.

g. Inform applicants that their test results might be discussed in case they are selected as finalists. Make them feel relaxed about it and always clearly state that a hiring decision is never made based on test results only.

CONDUCTING REFERENCE CHECKS _____

The value of reference checks. Reference checks are essential in verifying a candidate's background. Combined with the proper interviewing technique, as presented earlier in this book, reference checks should give you added assurance that the feeling you had about an applicant's abilities to successfully perform in the position is well-founded. It can also confirm some doubts or negative impressions about specific job-related performance or even soft skills.

Checking an applicant's references should, at a minimum, involve a factual investigation of education and employment. When calling educational institutions, ask for the records department and provide the applicant's social security number. Simply request the year the candidate attended classes and the graduation date. Verification of employment dates and job titles can be obtained by contacting prior employers.

Conducting reference checks with prior employers should be done after the first interview, when you have already decided to invite an applicant for a second, more thorough meeting. Getting this information prior to the second interview will provide you with valuable data that you can eventually use to challenge the applicant with.

Legal considerations. Reference checking can be a frustrating exercise that yields little useful information about a candidate. In light of recent court judgments against companies that either provided too much or not enough information about former employees, most firms are reluctant to do more than verify title, dates of employment and salary. Yet in the last few years, more states have passed laws providing immunity from liability to employers who want to provide references. Generally, courts are giving companies more protection from defamation suits, holding that the reference process is privileged.

You might not always obtain useful information when it comes to checking an applicant's references with a former employer, but it is worth to try, as this is often one of the best ways to discover the truth. You can increase the legal protection of all parties involved by doing the following:

- Obtain written permission from the applicant. Include a waiver in your application form and get it signed for approval of a third-party reference and background check.

- Ask for references. Formally request that each applicant provides at least 3 references from previous employers – names and contact information. Mention that no further consideration will be given to applicants who either do not provide references or do not sign the waiver form.

- List the questions. Openly inform applicants of the questions you intend to ask. Get applicants' signed approvals. You will be able to provide proof of permission to former employers who are reluctant to answer your queries.

- Get legal support. Send your question list above to your legal advisor for review prior to using it. Your state may have specific laws applying to reference checking. And the fact that a lawyer has approved the question list will make it easier for a former employer to provide the data.

Questions to ask when checking references. Remember the next few rules: your questions must relate to the position for which you are hiring; you should follow the same procedure for every applicant; do not take note of any comment unrelated to the specific job opening. Most importantly: get fact-based data, not opinions. Here are some questions you can ask. Again, consult your legal advisor before you formalize the question list:

- When did [applicant] start and end work at your company?
- What was his/her exact job description and responsibilities?
- What was his/her measurable performance on that job?
- What hard skills (technical or administrative) were needed on the job and did he/she demonstrate them?
- What soft skills were needed on the job and did he/she demonstrate them satisfactorily?
- What would you say his/her best qualities arc?
- How did he/she contribute to the group?
- Why did [applicant] leave the company?
- Did you offer career development to [applicant]? If not, why not?
- Would you rehire [applicant]?
- We are considering offering [applicant's name] a position as _____ (title of job), which requires a strong _____ (specific soft skill). Per your experience, how would you rate him/her on that specific skill (from 1 to 10)? (Repeat if more skills are needed).

When hiring a manager, ask the following additional questions:

- How would you describe [applicant]'s management style?
- What major achievement did he/she demonstrate as an executive for your company?
- What type of environment does [applicant] best perform in?
- The concerned job opening will require strong leadership aptitudes. How would you rank [applicant] on this, from 1 to 10?
- What are [applicant]'s three most valuable qualities?

Final notes. we recommend that you or the hiring manager directly contact former employers. A business owner will talk more freely to another business owner. Consider former employers as extremely important customers who are about to give you a feedback on the value of your services. Customer's advice is worth its weight in gold!

NO-FAIL HIRING TIPS

⮑ Right after the first interview, score your first impressions for each applicant. Determine what attributes you were able to clearly observe, both related to an applicant's hard and soft skills. You also need to question and focus on those attributes you were NOT able to detect that are important for optimal job effectiveness.

⮑ Use the "interview first impression table" and "applicant report form" to formalize your observations. Remember, the same standard forms need to be used for every interviewed candidate.

⮑ Good tests can reveal skills and capabilities that you might not obtain from an application or an interview. Such tests can also lower the incidence of theft and work-related accidents and help reduce the likelihood of negligent-hiring cases. Use professionally-developed tests that are proven to measure what they pretend to. And stay away from any psychological tests that investigate job-unrelated areas such as privacy, religious beliefs, sexual orientation, etc.

⮑ Our No-Fail Hiring System offers the *Recru-Tec Test*™, a unique online assessment. More than a personality test, it is a reactivity test that measures, through 20 different traits, an applicant's potential to deal with specific work conditions. This tool is available only as part of our overall hiring system and strongly contributes to removing doubts on critical soft skills such as honesty, loyalty, ability to work under pressure, communication and leadership skills, persistence, stability, self-confidence, etc. It is adverse-impact-proof and does not discriminate in any manner. It can be used for any position. Visit www.nofailhiring.com.

⮑ Combined with the proper interviewing technique, reference checking can be very effective to verify a candidate's background and to give more weight to your evaluation. Follow the procedure as presented in this chapter to avoid legal liabilities. Consider calling former employers yourself rather than delegating the task to an assistant.

Your second interview is really the revealing part of your hiring process, at the end of which you should feel entirely confident about your decision.

Chapter

10

Your Second Interview Scenario

HOW TO CONDUCT THE SECOND INTERVIEW

You have applied the three transitional steps to the second interview with your selected applicants – those who passed the first interview steps: (a) your first interview impressions, (b) any test results and (c) reference checks. These are strategic tools to be used either to separate the real top players from others or to challenge the finalists.

Do not forget to send every disqualified applicant a courteous letter of rejection. Avoid justifying the rejection with any opinion-driven comment or subjective evaluation but only with job-related reasons. This is a very important move: always clearly state the job-related–only reasons a candidate is not qualified to pursue the job application with your company.

We recommend that the fortunate contenders for a second interview be invited personally by the direct manager/supervisor and by the company business owner. Conducting this second interview is often a last step to "closing the deal"; having the top management present gives selected applicants a sense of importance. It is also a confirmed indicator of serious interest. Remember: qualified applicants are very aware of their value on the employment market.

The scenario for this second interview is simple and is based again on our favorite key word: challenge. You are indeed going to take up any unclear or uncertain issue discovered during each of the transitional steps.

You are also going to find out which direction each selected applicant is going, as a result of your strategically planned second meeting. Specifically, you want to challenge them on:

- Any weakness detected during the first interview as well as from test results,
- Feedback from former employers,
- Potential for career development (if applicable) and
- Conditions of employment (salary and other compensations).

CHALLENGING TEST RESULTS _____

The real value of testing. Good testing tools, especially personality assessments, offer extremely valuable information on an applicant's soft skills. That is, provided they are used intelligently and they passed the test of validity. But remember: test results should never be used separately in making a hiring decision. Rather, they should allow you to complement and challenge your observations about an applicant's strengths and weaknesses.

Also, keep in mind that most assessments confuse temporary personality with the chronic, permanent one. Detecting the "personality of the moment" is never going to provide valuable information, as you might find other, completely different personality traits once the person is on the job. Plus, it is well recognized that faking tests can be done and is actually a "natural" phenomenon among earthlings.

Per our experience and following research on faking, between 30 and 50% of job applicants elevate their scores on personality tests. Deceptive behavior is viewed as part of the competition for employment. Deception is often seen as a persuasion strategy, rather than pure dishonesty.

Most fakers would use deception as a means to achieve some desired purpose. During the process, the deceiver attempts to influence the beliefs and conclusions of his/her target – in this case, you.

The same research suggests that the fear of being caught is usually the best deterrent to faking. Alerting applicants that any evidence of cheating on tests will cancel the job application can diminish the desire to overly exaggerate one's scores.[2]

This means that the best value attached to candidates' testing is contained in your ability to challenge them on the results, rather than blindly trusting these results. And even more effective is the challenging of contradictory test results with your personal observations during the first interview. Unprepared reactions to your questions and challenges are indeed the most valuable predictors of future behavior.

How to deal with contradictions? There are many variables which can explain why personality test results would differ greatly from your thorough observations (besides the "halo" effect – see chapter 6):

- The chosen test is unreliable. You can avoid this by "testing the test" on some trusted, productive employees.

- The applicant completed the test under unfavorable conditions, such as being sick, tired, hungry or extremely stressed. You should always ensure that applicants complete tests under the best conditions. We recommend that you invite them to complete the selected test(s) while they are visiting your company, even if these tests are processed online. Do not trust applicants to complete a test from home.

- The applicant may present an unstable or "multi-masks" personality. You can suspect such a situation when an application shows a high degree of instability in the applicant's job history. This usually indicates how the applicant will behave in the future.

- If the applicant has tried to deceive the test, you can expect a critical reaction to your challenging questions. Just keep on challenging more and "force" the critical reaction.

How do you challenge test results? The way to challenge an applicant against your observations and the test results is simple. Challenge the applicant on any <u>weaknesses</u> observed or detected through testing:

a) Pick up any strange or unexplained personality weakness and ask the person to give his/her own viewpoint.

b) Ask the following question: "Give us an instance in a past job when you had to deal with such _____ [lack of soft skill]. What happened and how did you manage the situation?" You can also ask the same question if the applicant disagreed with the observed or reported weakness.

Pick up a few specific soft skills that were either observed or reported through testing and challenge the applicant. Note the reactions; they very often provide more data than the answers alone.

Remember: if you are not happy with an answer, challenge more. This is how you trigger a natural, unprepared reaction.

The next step is to challenge the applicant on positive soft skills or person-ality strengths, as observed or detected through testing. You want to get direct evidence of those positive attributes:

a) Pick up one positive personality attribute that is important for the job opening.

b) Ask the following question: "The personality test revealed that you do have great _____ [specific skill]. Please give us an instance when you had to demonstrate such an aptitude on the job?"

You can ask this question for more than one job-related personality strength.

CHALLENGING REFERENCE CHECKS _____

Dealing with positive feedback. Always start by acknowledging any positive feedback provided by a former employer. The applicant deserves it, provided the feedback was honest and fact-based. Specifically, address those positive attributes that are vital for the specific job opening. Remember, people work for people, not for businesses. By acknowledging positive feedback, you demonstrate a sense of importance for those attributes, as well as good leadership.

Using data from the company and job descriptions (see chapter 4), ask the following question:

"How do you believe _____ [quality as confirmed by former employer] will help you achieve the expected results on the job as well as contribute to our company's growth ambitions?"

DID YOU KNOW?

THE RECRU-TEC TEST™: A PERFECT COMPANION TO YOUR HIRING INTERVIEW

The RECRU-TEC TEST is the perfect quality control support to provide your hiring missions with the best outcome. Based on more than 22,000 candidates' evaluations, this unique assessment is a "job-matching" test which provides vital data about your potential new employees. The RECRU-TEC TEST helps you avoid costly mistakes and problems, by providing "hidden" data on the evaluated person which are essential to success on the job.

- It is a PRODUCTIVTY test. It detects a candidate's personality traits which may be deterrents to optimal job performance.

- It is a REACTIVITY test. It measures how the evaluated person will react to job-related circumstances, in a given work environment.

- It is a PREDICTION test. It helps you predict how the evaluated person will behave under specific job-related situations which require precise qualities and skills to resolve. This unique tool will reveal, with up to 90% precision, the applicant's natural reactions, decisions and actions to important job-related challenges.

Visit www.nofailhiring.com for more information.

You can ask the same question for any important positive attribute reported by a former employer.

Dealing with negative feedback. If you have received any plausible negative comment from a former employer, you also want to challenge the applicant about it. Such negative comment should be factual; however you want to get the applicant's side of the story. You can ask:

"We received a negative feedback from a former employer regarding _____ [specific lack of hard or soft skill]. Can you tell us about the circumstances where this was observed by your former employer?" Upon the applicant's answers, follow up by asking:

"How would you manage to overcome this lack of [specific skill], knowing that this skill is important to perform well on the job?"

You can ask the same question for any negative attribute reported by a former employer. Again, observe the applicant's reactions to the question, as it will provide great indications on his/her ability to manage such reported weaknesses, or not.

CHALLENGING DEVELOPMENT POTENTIAL

There are two main reasons why you want to inquire into an applicant's vision about the long-term future. First, it is a proven fact that people who can "see themselves" in the long term, are more liable to persist and fight through challenges. Second, a young hire might quickly develop into one of your executives within a few years, after having proven to be a high performing colleague on the job.

Some ambitious applicants will indeed "buy" a future promotion and will gladly take the current vacant position to prove (to you and to themselves) that they can do it – considering it is "just" a step toward a more challenging but rewarding level of responsibility.

A golden rule regarding future promotion. Never promise a future position when you hire for a current one. Make it extremely clear that any future promotion entirely depends on performance on the current job. Never offer that future job as part of your employment-at-will agreement.

Remember the rules of employment-at-will: even if there is a potential promotion at some future point, make it clear that the employment remains at-will and any promise or suggestion of future promotion will NOT change the nature of the employment agreement. Better yet: put it in writing (see chapter 2).

If you plan to hire high-potential employees, you want to get a good idea of what they have in mind in regards to the future. They may show great promises for performance on the immediate job, but how do you estimate how they will do in a future executive or higher-responsibility position?

You can't can predict the future that far ahead. But once you have determined that an applicant can potentially fill the vacant position, you can at least evaluate how he/she would rate doing that potential, future job!

Future-oriented questions to ask. Here again, our favorite key word applies. Challenge the applicant on the future, specifically on his/her viewpoint as to why he/she would deserve a promotion – or not!

For example, you can ask questions such as:

- "What are your professional ambitions in the next 3 to 5 years?"

- "To what extent do you think that this company can help you achieve these goals?"

- "What do you think would make you entitled to a promotion within our company in the future?"

    The answer should obviously demonstrate that the applicant understands a promotion entirely depends on performance on the job plus contribution to the team or group. When the applicant answers, follow up with:

- "Why should we trust you about the future?"

- "Is there any environmental factor which could prevent you from being able to assume more responsibility in the future?"

A good way to measure an applicant's real level of interest in a future higher position is to present the challenges related to that position as if he/she would need to take it up today. Present it under the form of a current challenge and submit a simulated situation. Get the applicant's feedback on how he/she would manage it – knowing that the simulation does not pertain to the current position.

Important notes:

Remember that the selected applicants had to "survive" through the first interview questions. Lying during this second interview would be quite visible, particularly after the "honesty test" they endured during the first meeting. Do not hesitate to challenge the applicant's answers and reactions further to provoke a natural, unprepared response.

Something else to remember is that you should not ask any questions related to the applicant's private life. Knowing if the applicant is planning to have a family and kids can be a vitally important piece of information if the applicant is supposed to travel a lot; but you can't ask! Rather, ask if the applicant will be able to accommodate a tenuous schedule and travelling, in the event of a future promotion. The applicant's reaction will tell you what to expect. Invite them to ask questions that will lead to knowing the real answers to your future-oriented questions!

CHALLENGING FINANCIAL CONDITIONS _____

When is it best to talk about it? As recommended in chapter 6, you should always provide general information on salary and other compensations in your job description. Making this clear to applicants at the beginning of the hiring process usually allows you to avoid wasting time with candidates who want to get rich fast, no matter how they are performing.

Another effective approach to the salary issue is to suggest that applicants describe their salary requirements either in a cover letter or in their job application.

If an applicant addresses the issue during the first interview, remember that it is best to brush off the subject and dedicate more time with selected candidates who can demonstrate their value during the second interview. Always take note of the applicant's question and ask them what they are expecting, if it wasn't addressed yet. This will let you know what negotiating position you want to take.

During the second interview, try to address the subject of salary and other compensations last. The applicant knows about the salary range anyway. He/she should be a bit patient about the details. The key point is: is he/she attracted by the job BEFORE you talk about money? Remember the exchange factor: money is important, but should not be the main reason for someone to take a job.

What is a competitive salary? There are as many answers to that question as there are jobs available on the market. You definitely should be competitive if you are looking to attract high performers. Your top players are aware of their value and will want to defend their competitiveness.

Our recommendation. Whomever you hire, we believe you should increase performance-based compensation. Trend indicators seem to agree on this issue. A poor economy and a strong need to remain competitive requires you to recruit dedicated, performing employees who are willing to be rewarded for their performance rather than for their presence. Doing otherwise opens the door to lower productivity.

Although it is quite obvious to compensate salespeople on performance, you can find some sort of bonus system for administrative or managerial positions. If you have defined a clear performance expectation for a job opening, one sure way to help new employees fight to reach their targets is to award the achievement, rather than the daily tasks. Employees tend to obtain what the manager pushes.

Money is not everything, but it certainly contributes to making people proud of their achievements. There is no better "People Management" strategy than to focus on target achievement and rewarding games with, among other things, a stake of the company's profits.

DID YOU KNOW?

**PERSISTING SLUGGISH ECONOMY WILL
DRIVE PERFORMANCE-BASED PAY**

According to The Conference Board Annual Salary Increase Budgets Survey Report, the U.S. salary increase budgets remain historically low and projections for 2011 show a very modest increase. For the second straight year, the median salary increase budget in 2010 is 2.5%. Projections for 2011 show a modest increase to 3%.

Across all industries, the 2011 forecast for salary increase budgets showed little variation, with no employee group in any industry projected to exceed the overall median of 3 percent. [3]

According to Tom McMullen, Hay Group's North American Reward Practice Leader, the contraction in the U.S. economy continues to cause US businesses to exercise restraint in growing base salaries.

"HR executives are looking for ways to balance the cost of reward programs and limited pay increases with the need to attract, retain and engage key talent," McMullen added. "While there isn't a significant shift in pay increases for the coming year, the mix of that pay is changing. As organizations emerge from the recession, they are shifting more focus from fixed to variable pay. This is partly cost-driven, as those organizations with higher proportions of variable pay tend to have more flexibility to cope with economic volatility. Variable pay has also proven to be an effective lever for motivating performance and aligning employees with the organization's goals and priorities," he said. [4]

YOUR SECOND INTERVIEW REPORT FORM

At the end of the second interview, you should be in a position to either decide to hire the selected applicant(s) or have a management coordination meeting, in order to make the final decision amongst finalists. We recommend that you formally evaluate this second meeting as you did with the first one.

You can develop a second interview summary form such as the following:

SECOND INTERVIEW REPORT FORM

NAME:_____   Date: _____   Position: _____

	High	Good	Fair	Low
1) Test results/Soft skills	____	____	____	____
2) Reference checks results	____	____	____	____
3) Development potential results	____	____	____	____
4) Financial conditions results	____	____	____	____
5) Motivation/Intentions	____	____	____	____
6) General impression at end	____	____	____	____

(Write down job-related-only notes that can support your own impression above.)

FINAL STEP:

When you have completed the second interview report form for each selected applicant, there is one more vital step you need to get them through, before you actually make your hiring decision. This last step should be considered your ultimate insurance policy against bad or negligent hiring. Let us see what needs to be done now to give your company the best probability of a happy, effective and objective recruitment procedure.

NO-FAIL HIRING TIPS

⮕ Your second interview scenario is to challenge selected applicants against (a) any weaknesses detected during the first interview and from their test results, (b) former employers' reference checks, (c) their potential for career development, and (d) employment financial conditions.

⮕ If you plan to use personality assessments, ensure they "pass the test" by using them first on trusted employees. This "benchmarking" will provide a much stronger evidence of validity and reliability than any statistical reports provided by the test developers.

⮕ Do not blindly rely on test results, rather use them to challenge the applicant on any contradiction or unexpected weakness. Get trained on the specific test evaluation – do not trust any provider who would refuse to educate you on their tool's "secrets."

⮕ Check our "reactivity" test, the RECRU-TEC TEST at www.nofailhiring. com. This unique assessment precisely measures 20 main personality-related traits which provide invaluable information on more than 50 soft skills, desired or needed for optimal performance for any position.

⮕ Challenge selected applicants on references provided by former employers. Do not hesitate to present negative comments from your checks to give the applicant a chance to give his/her side of the story. Remember: the reaction to a question provides more valuable information than the answer itself.

⮕ Next, challenge the applicants on their development potential – if applicable. You want to find out how the applicant is planning the next three to five years. A good vision of the future is a great indicator of stability, persistence and consistency.

⮕ Last, challenge the applicants on their financial requirements. This is a negotiation issue. If you want to pay someone more than originally planned, link the higher pay to performance, not to status or background. Beware of applicants who do not accept the idea of performance-based pay or bonuses.

Background checks constitute your best insurance policy against the potential liabilities of bad or negligent hiring. They can also provide additional data on needed hard and soft skills. Seriously, you should never hire anyone without using such a valuable resource.

Chapter

11

Background Checks: Your Top Insurance

"The challenge for organizations will be to ensure they get high quality background checks and use them routinely in a climate where untruthful resumes seem more common and the risks of bad hiring are greater."

Nick Fishman,
CEO of *EmployeeScreenIQ.* [1]

WHAT IS A BACKGROUND CHECK? _____

A background check is an organized way to find important information about someone that may not be readily available. It is usually conducted through third party institutions and has the purpose of providing a precise picture of an individual's character or qualifications based on past actions and records. In a study conducted in May 2010 by *EmployeeScreenIQ*, a global employment screening company based in Cleveland, Ohio, revealed that 92% of surveyed companies perform background checks. Of that majority, 70% use them for over 80% of the hires. Nearly all respondents (96%) agreed that candidates accepted the need for background checks.[2]

Though traditionally requested on candidates seeking a job requiring high security or a position of trust (such as in schools, hospitals, financial institutions, airports, and governments), these checks are routinely used today by smaller employers. They provide a means of objectively evaluating a job candidate's qualifications and of identifying potential hiring risks for safety and security reasons.

Background checks commonly include searches of employment, criminal, financial, driving and education records. For hiring purposes, employers should request precise information, including:

- verification of academic credentials,
- verification of prior employment (including position, longevity, salary, and job performance, sometimes tracing back ten years or to the three prior positions),
- verification of letters of recommendation or reference checks,
- drug screenings and physical exams (if applicable),
- an Internet search on a candidate's name,
- criminal background checks,
- credit checks,
- social security number,
- driver's license record.

WHY YOU SHOULD USE
BACKGROUND CHECKS

Predicting the future with the past. Background checks give you access to data from an applicant's past of which he/she would not necessarily want to talk about. By comparing data provided through a background check with the information obtained from the job application and during the two interviews, you are more likely to detect any falsification by the applicant.

This does not necessarily mean that background checks always tell the truth or provide fully accurate data. But again, any contradictory information is a source of challenge. For example, you should demand that applicants account for any discrepancy between credential provided in the background check and what they reported in their application.

Important note: do not blindly reject an applicant because of contradictory or un-matching information. Many providers do their best to collect data as accurately as possible, but these data collections are processed by human beings – so mistakes can be expected. The rule is: always use such data to challenge the concerned applicant first.

Aside from potential administrative mistakes, a background check will usually confirm or strengthen your observations and evaluation of an applicant. So it is, together with accurate testing, a great quality control on your prediction efforts.

Avoiding painful legal trouble. Not performing background checks on new (and sometimes existing) employees could open the door to serious legal risks! In at least 28 states, Negligent Hiring and Retention Laws hold employers liable for willful misconduct by their employees. In some cases, it does not matter if the employee's actions occur outside the course and scope of employment (See chapter 2).

Failure to screen current and prospective employees for criminal history and substance abuse can cost your company millions of dollars as well as huge damages to your customer relations! According to *Liability Consultants, Inc.*, the current average settlement in negligent hiring cases is $1.6 million.[3]

Lawsuits have been steadily increasing in the last 10 years. You definitely want to protect your company against potential legal sharks or criminal applicants who could become your worst nightmare.

Per *Reference Check,* a reference check service company, demonstrating that an employee was unfit for a particular job is one of the key elements in claiming that the employer was negligent. The most common criterion used to demonstrate that an employee is unfit for a particular position is evidence of past criminal or inappropriate behavior. Background checks provide critical data to avoid trouble.

Many examples of negligent hiring cases were given in Chapter 2. Here are a few more. As reported by *Reference Check,* most could have been avoided with the proper use of reference or background checks: [4]

- A fast food chain was sued for $200,000 when a worker assaulted a three-year old child and it was discovered that the individual had a criminal record that included assault.

- A suit was filed for $5 million against a property management company when a manager used a pass key to gain access to an apartment and sexually assaulted the tenant. The management company settled out of court when it was discovered that the manager had been convicted of apartment burglary several years before.

- One employer was liable for a road accident caused by one of his truck drivers who had lied about his experience, had several speeding tickets and had no training as a truck driver.

Avoiding violence and crime at work. Background checks can help you detect individuals who are prone to violent or criminal conduct, thus avoiding negligent hiring liabilities. Violence at work can indeed be a serious justification for employees or outside victims to sue for damages.

Per a National Crime Victimization Survey, almost 2 million individuals become victims of work-related violent crimes every year. Crime victimization in the workplace costs employers about 1,751,100 lost workdays each year, averaging 3.5 days per crime. These missed days of work result in more than $55 million in lost wages annually. This figure does not include the cost of sick days and annual leave. When compensatory and punitive damages from negligent hiring lawsuits are added to the above figures, damages in a single case may cost an employer a great deal of money.[5]

As reported by the American Management Association, U.S. companies experience significant losses due to employee misconduct: [5]

- Employee Pilferage over $10 billion.

- Commercial Bribery over $10 billion.

- Embezzlement over $4 billion.

- Vandalism over $2.5 billion.

- Burglary over $2.5 billion.

- Insurance/Workers' Compensation Fraud over $2 billion.

- Arson over $1.3 billion.

- Computer Fraud over $1 billion.

DID YOU KNOW?

- A National Crime Victimization Survey reported that each year, over two million U.S. residents become victims of work-related violence. [7]

- The National Institute of Occupational Safety and Health found that 20 persons were murdered at work every week. Nationally, homicide is the second highest overall cause of workplace-related deaths; for female workers, homicide is the leading cause of workplace deaths.[8]

  Workplace violence now accounts for 15% of the more than 6.5 million violent acts experienced by U.S. residents who are age 12 or older.[9]

According to *Consumer Credentials*, an employment screening and background check firm, criminal behavior is not the only threat to your business: substance abuse can also lead to significant damages and monetary loss. As reported by the National Clearinghouse for Drug and Alcohol Abuse: *"No business regardless of size is immune to the countless problems that alcohol and drug abuse can cause. Workplace alcohol, tobacco, and other drug related problems cost U.S. companies over $100 billion each year."*[6]

THE LEGAL ASPECT OF BACKGROUND CHECKS

Obligation of information and consent. The use of background checks for employment purposes is regulated by the Fair Credit Reporting Act (FCRA). The FCRA sets the standards for employment screening and defines a background check as a consumer report. Before your company can obtain a consumer report or run a credit check for employment purposes, you must notify the applicant in writing and get his/her written authorization. Even if you are simply conducting inquiries (rather than running reports), you should still ask for the applicant's consent (see chapter 2).

If you decide not to hire as a result of a background check report, you must give the rejected applicant a pre-adverse action disclosure that includes a copy of the report and a copy of his/her rights. You should then give the applicant notice that you have decided not to hire them and let them know the name and address of the Consumer Reporting Agency. Also include information on their right to dispute the background check report.

Disclosure limits. Some information cannot be disclosed under any circumstances in background checks. For example, school records are confidential and cannot be released without the consent of the student. Applicants cannot be discriminated against because they filed for bankruptcy. Laws vary on checking criminal history. Some states don't allow questions about arrests or convictions beyond a certain point in the past. Others only allow consideration of criminal history for certain positions.

You cannot request medical records and may not make hiring decisions based on information about an applicant's disability. You may only inquire about an applicant's ability to perform a certain job. The same holds true for Workers' Compensation. The military can disclose an applicant's name, rank, salary, assignments and awards without consent. Driver's license records are not confidential either and can be released without consent as they are public records.

The Equal Employment Opportunity Commission (EEOC) considers that you cannot automatically disqualify an applicant because of a past criminal record. You can weigh such factor in your overall evaluation, but you must have a sound business reason for not hiring someone with a conviction. In other words, the criminal conviction is NOT by itself a sufficient reason not to not hire an applicant. You still must be able to justify your decision with job-related arguments in disfavor of an applicant. For example, you could not justify refusal to hire an accountant who was convicted for multiple traffic violations.

The law may vary in different states, so make sure you check with your attorney about what can be done with background checks and under which conditions. Some states have actually passed laws to protect employers who do their due diligence.

For example, Florida House Bill H775 (passed in 1999), provides protection for employers against negligent hiring liabilities, provided they attempt to conduct certain screening procedures. Employers who follow the following steps will be presumed to not have been negligent when hiring if a background check fails to reveal records on an applicant: [10]

- Ordering a Florida State criminal record check.
- Taking reasonable efforts to contact an applicant's past employers.
- Asking the applicant on the application if they have been convicted of a crime, date of crime and penalty imposed.
- Asking the applicant on the application if they were the defendant in a civil action for intentional tort.
- Ordering a driving record if it is relevant to the performed work.
- Interviewing the applicant.

Potential legal liabilities. Avoid trying to reduce costs related to background checking by relying solely on a variety of national criminal databases to perform your pre-employment screenings. Catherine Aldrich, former executive vice-president for *Accurate Background, Inc.*, cautions that most of these databases contain incomplete criminal records from less than 28% of the counties in the United States, and that they often include listings of traffic violations that have little value for pre-employment screening purposes.[11]

Moreover, these databases are updated and maintained in a manner that may generate errors and partial record information not suitable for making the best hiring decisions, considered not compliant with the FCRA.

In her article *"The Devil Inside — Legal Liabilities of Background Screening,"* Aldrich provides the following example of the legal limits and liabilities attached to background-checking:[12]

A major bank requested a routine criminal background check on an applicant applying for a teller position in Wisconsin and found that he had felony convictions for rape and sexual assault. Following established hiring procedures, the hiring manager informed the applicant of these findings and swiftly rejected his application for further employment.

Soon after, the applicant filed a wrongful hiring discrimination lawsuit. The bank defended the action vigorously but was found to have violated fair hiring laws and was ordered to pay a judgment of more than $1 million as well as offer the sex offender employment within the company. The court found that the bank had ignored local restrictions stating that an employer could only consider prior criminal convictions that were significantly related to the performance of the applicant's prospective job.

The court ruled that since a bank teller working behind a security partition would never be in physical contact with customers, there was no possibility for assault or rape during the conduct of his job. Therefore, the bank could not use the prior felony convictions in its hiring deliberations.

As a reminder: never make your final hiring or rejection decision solely based on background check results. Always clearly demonstrate that a criminal or violent background can jeopardize job performance and/or can be a liability for the safety of other employees and customers or even any related third parties.

The key issue here is: the rejection must be job-related. Ensure that your job description clearly mentions (if applicable) the importance of a crime, violence and/or drug-free background, and demonstrate why it is important to acceptable performance on the job.

WHAT TO LOOK FOR IN A BACKGROUND-CHECKING PROVIDER

Regardless of the level of service, you should make sure that the chosen provider complies with all federal and state laws governing employment background checks. Your provider should be able to demonstrate its knowledge of the FCRA and equal employment opportunity law as well as other federal and state regulations that address employment background checks. It should also be able to demonstrate compliance procedures in place in its company.

Ensure that your attorney is familiar with the FCRA. Ask him/her to review your service agreement, making sure that it specifically describes the services provided, liability, and the compliance roles of the parties involved (see chapter 3 for details).

A serious background-checking company will require you to have an applicant-signed release authorizing the background check before conducting its search. The FCRA requires that a provider shall not conduct a background check without having primarily obtained this authorization.

You should also ask the provider about the legality of its data sources. You don't want to be the recipient of illegally obtained information. Any privacy-related data is forbidden. Ask your provider to tell you how they deal with private information and you will get a good idea of their professionalism.

Some other points to verify with a potential background-checking service provider:

- Can it show evidence of compliance with all federal and state requirements, including its current license?

- Can it provide all the data needed to make a decision based on your specific hiring criteria?

- Can it provide a report in a timely manner?

- Does it have a national or regional scope?

- Can it provide regulatory guidance (especially about the FCRA)?

DEFINING YOUR BACKGROUND CHECK POLICY

You should have a background check policy as part of your general hiring policy. You want to clearly describe the way that background checks are handled for all current and prospective employees. A background check policy could state the following information:

- Prior to or upon an employee's acceptance of an offer for employment, [your company] has a policy of systematically conducting a background check on every selected applicant.

- Any job offer with [your company] is conditional on the required background check reports, to the degree that such reports may reveal information deterrent to acceptable job performance.

- Every selected applicant shall sign an acceptance form, allowing [your company] to perform background checks. Refusal of acceptance will lead to an automatic cancellation of the application or termination of employment, if a background check report is found to be detrimental to the job and our company.

- Such employment background check may provide information related to prior employment, professional experience and education, personal or professional references, professional certifications, driving record, and criminal background.

- As deemed appropriate by [your company], further background checks may be conducted. Employment may be subject to the findings of one or more completed background checks.

- Every selected applicant undergoing a background check has a right to access reports. In case a background check report leads to a decision to not hire an applicant, such applicant will receive a copy of the report and the contact information of [your company] background check provider.

It is also suggested that you formalize your background check reports and findings for every selected applicant. Depending on the specific job, you could use a summary table similar to the following:

DID YOU KNOW?

FIND A LOCAL BACKGROUND CHECKING SERVICE PROVIDER ONLINE

The **National Institute for the Prevention of Workplace Violence** provides a nationwide list of pre-employment background screening companies. It is a fast and easy guide to finding a background screening service to use when you plan to conduct investigative checks on potential employees. [13]

In addition, the **National Association of Professional Background Screeners** (www.napbs.com), which is the voice of the background screening industry, also has a list of members. We urge employers to look for membership in the national professional association since it demonstrates a commitment to professional standards.

To have access to a full list of 40 questions to ask a pre-employment background screening firm, visit **Employment Screening Resources** at www.esrcheck.com/ESRadvantage.php.

BACKGROUND CHECK REPORT FORM

Applicant's Name: _____   Date: _____

Job applied for: _____

- Academic credentials conform to resume/job application   Yes __ No __
- Prior employment data conforms to resume/job application   Yes __ No __
- Prior salary data conforms to resume/job application   Yes __ No __
- Credit check data meets acceptable job requirements   Yes __ No __
- Social security number conforms to data provided   Yes __ No __
- Driver's license record conforms to data provided   Yes __ No __
- Report is clear of violent or criminal background   Yes __ No __
- If reports shows violent or criminal background, it
  conforms to data provided by applicant   Yes __ No __
- Criminal background check is acceptable for job   Yes __ No __
- If criminal background check is not acceptable for job, provide
  specific reasons why (only job-related reasons):

_____

_____

_____

_____

_____

_____

_____

_____

Note: always check with your attorney before using any report form.

NO-FAIL HIRING TIPS

➲ Background checks constitute your best insurance policy against potential liabilities related to bad or negligent hiring. They are also a reliable source of vital data regarding needed hard and soft skills. You risk much more by not using them on your finalist applicants.

➲ The primary reason to use background checks is to predict an applicant's honesty, future performance potential and loyalty, by cross-checking his/her resume or application data with the information released through the checks. Past performances more than often dictate future ones.

➲ Another strong reason to use background checks is legal protection. Many states hold employers responsible for willful misconduct by their employees. Negligent hiring cases are on the rise and employment regulations are getting tougher for small businesses. Even the employment-at-will law has recently been the subject of aggressive reform attempts from the EEOC. Make a good use of pre-employment screening. Do not try to save money on cheap screening services.

➲ One more reason to use background checks is to lessen the odds of violence at work. Violence often leads to legal trouble and can jeopardize the morale of your troops as well as your customer relationship. Pre-employment screening helps you detect convicted bullies before you offer them jobs.

➲ Get well-educated on the federal and state regulations associated with background checking. Even if you use outside service providers, you still need to comply with tough FCRA-related rules on the use of background checks. If you decide to use a screening firm — which we recommend — make sure that part of their service is offering educational assistance.

➲ Not every background-checking company is the same. Ensure you do your due diligence before retaining one. Use the list in this chapter to investigate the relevance and quality of their services. If they fail to follow the reporting regulations, you may be held liable for any violation of the concerned laws – and for the consequences of any related legal harassment.

The most serious challenge of hiring is to remove fate and luck from the outcome of your decision. Prediction is the key word and can only be achieved or approximated by reducing subjectivity to a minimum.

Chapter

12

Picking Your Top Players

"Hiring good people is hard. Hiring great people is brutally hard. Yet nothing matters more in winning than getting the right people on the field, then guiding them on the right way to succeed and get ahead."

Jack Welch,
former GE CEO,
Author of *"Winning."* [1]

PUTTING IT ALL TOGETHER _____

Objectivity rules. A sure way to objectively evaluate finalists is to score each of them against a standard list of criteria. This is the best strategy to avoid legal trouble as the evaluation criteria are the same for every applicant. And even if only one candidate remains, do the drill; it will naturally force you to put aside any subjective feelings or opinions. Your applicant evaluation summary table could look like this:

APPLICANT EVALUATION SUMMARY TABLE

NAME _____ JOB APPLIED FOR _____

DATE _____ MANAGER'S NAME _____

		Excellent	Good	Fair	Poor
•	Job application/resume	___	___	___	___
•	Phone pre-screening	___	___	___	___
•	First interview:				
–	Past performance/track record	___	___	___	___
–	Future performance potential	___	___	___	___
–	Willingness	___	___	___	___
–	Know-how	___	___	___	___
–	Personality/Soft skills	___	___	___	___
–	Motivation/Intentions	___	___	___	___
–	Own impression at end	___	___	___	___
•	Second interview:				
–	Test results – aptitude	___	___	___	___
–	Test results – soft skills	___	___	___	___
–	Reference check results	___	___	___	___
–	Development potential	___	___	___	___
–	Financial requirements	___	___	___	___

APPLICANT EVALUATION SUMMARY TABLE - Continued

    –   Motivation/Intentions   ___   ___   ___   ___

    –   General impression at end   ___   ___   ___   ___

- Background check(s)   ___   ___   ___   ___

- Specific <u>strengths</u> observed which are critical to job performance:

   _____

   _____

   _____

- Specific <u>weaknesses</u> which might be deterrents to job performance:

   _____

   _____

   _____

- General assessment, Interviewer no. 1:

   _____

   _____

   _____

- General assessment, Interviewer no. 2:

   _____

   _____

   _____

- **FINAL RECOMMENDATIONS:**

   _____

   _____

   _____

MAKING AND CLOSING THE JOB OFFER _____

Theoretically, each finalist applicant has accepted your "bottom line" employment conditions, specifically the salary range and other compensations. These issues were addressed in your second interview. Once you extend a formal job offer to a selected top player, chances are he/she will want to negotiate the details with you. Top players know their value and probably have more than one job offer to choose from.

Our observation is that top players receive, on average, 4 to 5 job offers during their job search. So when it comes to closing the deal, you must know that they will evaluate options to ensure that the total package is the most advantageous one for them. Remember the 4 evaluation criteria used by candidates to judge a potential employer (see chapter 3). In this chapter we are only considering the compensation package – often viewed as the make/break decision point.

Know what they are looking for. When it comes to money, your competitors will probably show an aggressive attitude in order to hire top players. And top players know it. Here is a checklist of options they usually look for when evaluating and negotiating a job offer:

- **Basic compensation**: Does your offer provide the applicant with a level of income that will at least enable him/her to maintain his/her current living standard?

- **Pay-per-performance**: Does your offer include a motivating variable part which will naturally lead the applicant to perform? Such a benefit should ideally include both individual and group performance-based commissions.

- **Bonuses and profit sharing**: Do you offer any bonus or profit-sharing programs for executive-type, higher level positions?

- **Performance & salary appraisals**: Do you have a policy about reviewing performance AND salary?

- **Career advancement opportunity**: Do you offer opportunities for career advancement and what criteria are used to evaluate such advancement?

- **Health insurance**: Do you offer it? Does the policy cover just the applicant or eligible dependants as well? How much of the premium do you pay?

- **Travel reimbursement**: If the applicant is required to travel, what is the policy regarding job-related expenses?

- **Relocation reimbursement**: If the job requires relocating, do you offer moving and/or relocation support?

- **Vacations and holidays**: How many paid holidays do you offer? What is the company's vacation policy?

- **Day care**: If applicable, do you offer any plan that can facilitate such service for your applicants' children?

- **Flextime**: Do you offer a flexible working schedule? If so, under what circumstances? Can applicants work from home?

- **Retirement**: Do you have a retirement plan? Is the applicant required to contribute to it? What are the conditions for accessing the funds in the applicant's retirement account?

- **Sick days**: Do you allow personal days or sick days? If so, how many and under what circumstances?

- **Maternity/family leave**: What is the company policy regarding maternity or family leave?

Negotiation tips. When you have decided to formally offer a job to a top player, it is recommended that you first prepare the negotiation. As stated earlier, this may take place during the second interview or after you have received the background check results and have presented your job offer – in which case you plan a third meeting with the selected applicant(s).

Here are a few tips to help you persuade a top player that the future is brighter with your company:

- Do not address the complete compensation package too early – you have provided information on the salary range in the job description so you should not fall into the trap of a premature salary negotiation. Ensure that you have ALL the data which will allow you to make an appropriate decision. A qualified applicant will most often want to negotiate with you. It may be worth it, but only if you have the needed data to judge.

- Be prepared to stress the other three job selection criteria: nature of the job, working environment and development potential (see chapter 3). These factors may and often do outweigh an immediate, more attractive salary.

- Stress the components of your compensation package which increase the applicant's quality of life. Many people are willing to take less pay if they recognize that the job and the company will contribute to higher living standards, less stress, more family time, etc. In any case, remember that the three job selection criteria above have power of influence against the compensation factor alone. And quality of life is a critical one.

- If you feel you need to compromise on the salary or you should satisfy a top player's higher request, try to attach the difference between your planned top level pay and his/her request to performance. In other words, do not increase the fixed part of the salary but rather make the compromised amount part of a variable commission or bonus, based on performance.

- Never offer what a selected applicant wants but always start a bit lower. Top players are expected to negotiate. Many of them will tell you that a competitor has already proposed more, no matter what you offer. So set the starting level of negotiation.

- Do your research. Find out what companies in your industry and your area are paying for similar jobs. Take advantage of the various national hiring consulting firms who can provide information on salaries per job category. If you plan to hire a top player who will relocate from an urban area while you are located in a suburban area, be prepared to show the difference in costs of living – and, again, quality of life. Search "salary," "wages" or "compensation" on Google and you will find a plethora of salary surveys and information – per job category and geographic area.

- Even if an applicant declines your offer, do not close the door. Invite him/her to visit you and try to obtain the specific reason for the decline. Obtain data on what benefits your "competitor" (another company offering a better salary and compensation plan) has provided, so that you can measure the reality of these.

- A bright, eager top player might send or present a counteroffer. Always try to find out if a competitor is really pushing the applicant's move or if it represents a self-originated action. Do not hesitate to ask who the other contender is and what the specifics of their job offer are. Challenge the applicant on the other three job selection factors. Ask for evidence of the proposal. If you are ready to compromise, always do so only after you have seen evidence of a higher global offer.

DID YOU KNOW?

**2010 UNEMPLOYED WORKERS
COMPLAIN JOB OFFERS PAY 25% LESS**

Although many unemployed workers are eager to start earning a paycheck, some are holding out for better offers. A new survey from *Personified*, CareerBuilder's talent consulting branch, shows that 17% of unemployed workers have received at least one job offer since they have become unemployed. Of these workers, 92% rejected the offer. 54% reported the pay was more than 25% below the salary they earned in their most recent position. The survey, which was conducted from August 4 to August 27, 2010, included 925 unemployed workers nationwide.[2]

DEFINING THE EMPLOYMENT RELATIONSHIP _____

Contract or no contract? Be advised that when you send a letter of offer or verbally present a job offer, it might constitute an employment contract. Per the law, an employment contract is an agreement between an employee and employer that specifies the terms of employment. It may be explicit or implied.

The safest way to avoid the potential liabilities attached to an employment contract is to start by clearly mentioning in the job offer that the employment is "at-will." Details on employment-at-will are given in Chapter 2. Make sure your attorney is well-educated on that subject.

Employment-at-will remains the small business preference when hiring employees. But times are changing and the doctrine has been a prime target of courts and the EEOC. We strongly suggest that you follow our practical tips on employment-at-will as given in Chapter 2. Do not get caught in the employment discrimination labyrinth by improperly stating the exact conditions of the employment-at-will relationship with a new employee.

Although over 70% of employees are employed at-will in the USA, an employment contract is sometimes to the employer's advantage. You might seek to have better control over an employee's ability to leave your business or you might need to have them on the job for a specific minimum period of time. Employment contracts might also make sense when the employee has to learn confidential and sensitive information about your business. You might then want to insert confidentiality clauses that prevent the employee from disclosing the data or using it for personal gain. A contract can also protect you by preventing an employee from joining a competitor immediately after leaving your company.

If you plan to hire an employee or executive with an employment contract, you will need to disclose important information in the contract which might legally help you in case of trouble, such as:

–   Job description with the employee's exact responsibilities and duties, as well as the expected attitude on the job.

- Salary and other compensations.

- Duration of the job (one year, two years, or indefinitely).

- Benefits (health insurance, vacation leave, etc.).

- An exact description of reasons for termination (make sure you include specific performance-monitoring statistics).

- Non-compete conditions when they leave your company.

- Protection of any trade secret and/or client lists.

Be aware that an employment contract infers a special obligation to deal fairly with the employee. If you end up treating an employee in a way that seems unfair, you may be legally responsible for not only violating the contract, but also for breaching your duty to act in good faith. Have your contract reviewed by your attorney.

Nondisclosure agreement. If you want to protect some trade secrets or confidential information regarding your business, you may want to require that employees sign a nondisclosure agreement, also called an NDA or a confidentiality agreement. It is a contract in which the parties promise to protect the confidentiality of secret information that is disclosed during employment or some other type of business transaction, inclusive of, but not limited to, clients, customer contacts, exclusive data and procedures.

Again, enlist your attorney's help to develop a written NDA that covers at least the following data:

- Definition of confidential information: provides details of which information is confidential and needs to be protected.

- Exclusions from confidential information: helps both parties to avoid confusions and/or mistakes of judgment.

- Obligations of employee: specifies that the employee cannot breach the confidential relationship, induce others to breach it, or induce others to acquire the confidential data.

- Time periods: 5 years is common in nondisclosure agreements.

- State of application: sometimes it is beneficial to specify which state law will apply in case the agreement is breached.

- Arbitration clause: you may want to specify the conditions of arbitration before a breach of contract is brought to court.

Non-compete agreement. Also known as a "covenant not to compete," a non-compete agreement is a promise by an employee not to compete with you for a specified time, in a particular place or in a particular way. You can make the signing of a non-compete agreement part of your terms of employment without creating an employment contract. It can be a separate document or part of your employment-at-will agreement form.

Non-compete agreements are hard to enforce. Many courts perceive them as attempts to limit an individual's ability to obtain employment. For that reason, most courts will insist that a non-compete agreement be reasonably limited in geographic scope and duration. The law varies from state to state so ensure that your attorney is well-informed on that sensitive subject.

If you feel a non-compete agreement is needed, ensure that your attorney considers some important criteria, such as:

- The non-compete should be clearly presented before you hire an employee. Some states such as Connecticut, Minnesota, Washington and Wisconsin require non-compete, nondisclosure or non-solicitation agreements to be presented to an employee before his/her first day of work, to ensure "sufficient consideration." In these states, employers cannot require existing employees to execute non-compete without additional consideration.

- Provide a good business reason for asking an employee to sign your agreement. It can't serve as a single purpose to punish an employee for leaving your company. If the reason is not clear, the legal system will scrutinize your agreement in case of a complaint. The main focus of employment law is to protect people's right to earn a living.

- Be specific in defining the confidentiality of information or knowledge. It can be in terms of equipment, data, technology, strategy, sales prospects, or other pertinent proprietary information or know-how. The more you specify it, the easier it will be for courts to determine its confidentiality.

– Do not be selective in imposing such an agreement. Every finalist applicant should be informed about it. Presenting it only to one person could be seen as discrimination.

– Provide some type of incentive or reward to any new employee who signs the agreement. This can be given under the form of bonuses or some special financial support to help the employee later find a new job with a non-competitor. Of course, make that reward conditional to the respect of the non-compete agreement.

– Do not require too long of a period of non compete, as you might violate the basic law of "right to earn a living." Many legal cases have been settled in favor of an employee who broke an agreement, justifying that they had to find a job in order to make a living. You will not easily win against such a case.

– California generally does not recognize non-compete agreements; however, you can use non-solicitation/nondisclosure agreements if you have to protect your trade secrets and/or client lists.

MANAGING REJECTED APPLICANTS _____

The most important consideration about finalist applicants who were not offered a job is that they still could become your employees sooner or later. You have spent tremendous time and energy to promote your vacant position. Hopefully you met with more than one very qualified applicant who could have taken the job. You made your decision based on YOUR appreciation and evaluation.

But here is the hard reality. Your chosen one might change his/her mind. He or she might suddenly receive a better offer. Or even worse: he/she might suddenly change attitude. Although your chances of success have doubled or tripled thanks to the application of our *No-Fail Hiring* procedure, recruitment has never been and will never be an exact science.

Within three to four weeks of having hired your new employees, you will be able to study and observe them. If you proceeded like most business owners do, you gave them a 30 to 90-day trial period, as clearly mentioned in the employment at-will agreement (the relationship remaining at-will after the trial period).

So, our golden rule is: always try to keep two to three finalists on the back burner. Communicate openly that they remain strong contestants for winning the job. Buy some time. Do not send a formal letter of rejection to those "reserves" yet. Keep a good relationship with them; call them on a weekly basis. Remember that over 70% of your applicants have a job. They might accept waiting a little longer before you inform them of the resolution of your search.

As for those who definitely will not take the job, remember that the world is a small one – especially on the Internet. Make sure that all applicants keep a happy memory of their visit. Whatever the outcome, you do not want to hear from a friend or an employee that some candidate posted a negative comment about an unsuccessful application. A personal phone call from your assistant followed by a friendly personal letter will remind the rejected applicant that you care enough. Think of what you should do to naturally motivate these rejected applicants to send you their friends…who could well qualify!

NO-FAIL HIRING TIPS

➲ Formalize your last step selection process with an *Applicant Evaluation Summary Table*, such as the one presented in this chapter. Even if only one candidate remains on the line, this will naturally "force" you to apply objective evaluation criteria, up to the end of the selection.

➲ Knowing what top players are expecting, prepare your negotiation prior to meeting finalist applicants. Follow our *Negotiation Tips* to ensure that you have done your due diligence. Top players know what they are worth and will not hesitate to negotiate with you the best conditions of their employment.

➲ Remember to be clear regarding your conditions of employment. In some states, the fact that no agreement was written with a new employee can lead to the existence of an implied contract. When you extend a job offer to a candidate, always ensure that you have specified, in writing, that the employment is at-will. Not mentioning it clearly could very well lead some legal authority to consider that such offer was acting as a contract.

➲ If you plan to hire an employee with an employment contract, you must disclose important information in the contract which might legally help you in case of trouble. Follow our recommendations presented in this chapter and submit your copy to your attorney for review.

➲ Nondisclosure agreements can be an effective way to protect your know-how and/or your trade secrets. The applicant's formal agreement by signature can be obtained separately from your at-will agreement. Likewise, non-compete agreements should be presented prior to start of work in order to minimize the potential of additional consideration, although in some states you have no choice.

➲ Our No-Fail Hiring System gives you a full procedure that allows you to keep optimal control, from the beginning to the end of a hiring mission. It guarantees to optimize the objectivity of your decision and to minimize the odds of making a costly mistake – organizationally and legally. Go to www.nofailhiring.com for more information.

Part D

The
Retention
Challenge

No matter how good or unique your product or service is, the success of your business depends entirely on your employees' passion, conviction and dedication. So consider your employees as your most important customers, because they are.

Chapter

13

Why New Employees Leave

> "'When an employee realizes that the employer cannot meet a key expectation in the contract, there is often a feeling of having been betrayed, as if a real contract has been broken in bad faith. This can become the 'shock' or turning point that begins the downward cycle toward disengagement and departure."
>
> **Leigh Branham**,
> *"The 7 Hidden Reasons*
> *Employees Leave"* [1]

FALSE EXPECTATIONS

A new employee comes to your office or calls you after 2 or 3 weeks on the job and announces his/her departure. When asked for the reason, the reply is almost the same each time: "It is just not what I was expecting, really."

While it is tempting to blame the departing employee for his/her decision, we always suggest that employers losing newly-hired staff re-examine their hiring process, particularly if this kind of turnover is a recurring problem. Applicants begin developing expectations about a position and a company at the first contact and definitely when they read the job description. If a job ends up being very different than what an employee anticipated, it's more than often because he/she received incorrect or incomplete information during the application process.

This is why you should always apply the rule of transparency: tell the truth when developing your job description and when talking to applicants. It is proven that employees who do not fully understand the scope of their work tend to leave their job soon after starting. Remember: while challenges will attract top players, they also will scare poor players away. This is what you want.

But do not attempt to sell a false, prettier picture of a position or the company in order to attract qualified, top players. They will punish you severely by leaving the company as soon as they find out. Honesty is a major selection criterion used by many applicants to judge you and your company. Top players do not tolerate lack of transparency.

In his excellent book, *"The 7 Hidden Reasons Employees Leave,"* Leigh Branham attributes the first reason for employee departures to unmet expectations. According to his research: [2]

- 4% of employees walk out of the job on the first day,

- 50% of American workers quit in the first 6 months,

- 40% of new executives fail to last more than 18 months in their new position.

Here are a few suggestions to help you minimize improper expectations and unwelcome surprises with freshly chosen top players:

- Ensure that your job description is complete and clear enough, without vague promise of a bright advancement – no matter what you offer on the current position.

- Insist on clarity about the job's existing situation. If the position was vacant for a long time, explain why. If the previous employee was fired, provide enough information so that the new player does not develop incorrect assumptions. Don't be overly negative about it but try to be realistic.

- Challenge them while presenting your personal (but realistic) picture of a bright future. Make sure that applicants understand what it will take to create that bright future.

- Honestly inform them about the "not-so-rosy" side of the job, during the interview. Provide a full reality of what the employee will face on a daily basis, once on the job.

- Ensure that the matching of a new employee with his/her manager will fit. If a new employee's direct supervisor is a tough person by nature, make sure that the employee will be able to live with it. Never hire someone without ensuring that he/she will accept the authority of a manager. On the other hand, if that manager is too tough for many, expect to lose a lot of top players during your hiring process. See why later in this chapter.

- Your company culture and management philosophy are vital selection criteria for top players. Do not play or present a flexible-type of culture during the hiring process and shift to a more rigid one after the hiring is complete. It won't take long before the new hire finds out you were "acting"!

- Prior to formally integrating a new employee into your team, have the person review the job description and the company's general employee policies. Such policies should illustrate your attention on developing and maintaining good, productive and inspiring employee relations. Ensure that the new employee understands the terms of employment and what attitude is expected in the company, as far as teamwork is concerned.

LACK OF ATTENTION

The second most visible reason behind losing new employees is lack of attention. Once on post, the new hire has to make it go right by himself/herself. It is rather remarkable that many employers evaluate their employees' competencies by how fast they can adapt to their new environments and job conditions – without looking at the consequences of their constant job-crisis handlings.

Although it is a good indicator of ability, being left alone from the start can open the door to many drawbacks. Our experience with customers' management challenges has shown that, when having to handle the job difficulties by themselves without anyone's help or support, they react differently – depending on their own personality:

- 20% of new employees find their way through and quickly develop a work pattern that fits well with your expectations.

- 20% of them lose control within less than 6 weeks and show unacceptable performance.

- 60% of them spend more time and energy trying to find out what needs to be done and how, rather than actually doing the job. They waste a lot of time, as well as their direct supervisor's and yours. Nobody is really happy. After a while, management starts to doubt about their employees' ability to make it go right.

- Some of them will remain on the job because they somehow were able to handle emergencies and important issues. But in the process they also developed inefficient work habits and/or inappropriate responses to difficult work conditions.

Losing an employee within the first 3 months of hiring can cost your company the equivalent of his/her yearly salary. Evaluate the frustrations and wasted time you and other executives suffered from losing one new employee and you will easily realize you should have spent more time with them in order to make them operational and happy on the job. All the efforts and "pain" incurred during the hiring process can be wasted in less than a few weeks, just because nobody was there to show enough attention. There are many areas where a new employee needs attention, some of which follow:

- Meeting colleagues in the company,
- Learning how to manage one's new boss,
- Getting oriented in the company,
- Finding out about the company's "unspoken" culture,
- Getting to know other people in other departments,
- Finding out who does what,
- Finding out how to do one's job,
- Finding out where to find help when needed,
- Finding out where to find tools and/or other material,
- Detecting who one can talk to when in trouble,
- Getting accustomed to the new working environment,
- Detecting who one's job depends on – besides one's boss,
- Getting accustomed to internal regulations,
- Feeling integrated as part of the team,
- Feeling happy to come to work every day,
- Knowing how to present a complaint or suggestion,
- Who to go to for a special recommendation or favor.

One critical element is worth mentioning separately: how much attention is given to developing a new employee's core competencies and know-how on the job. If you forget the rest above, this one would be *the* most vital attention grabber: what are you doing to make the new employee a more competent, more knowledgeable and more performing one, as fast as possible? What training have you planned?

This key question alone can make the whole difference about how the new employee feels, as most top players' first concerns are to quickly develop on their jobs and develop their future.

Some important aspects of personal development and training on (and outside) the job are:

- Providing the new employee with the necessary materials and documents that precisely describe his/her job.

- Having someone accompany the new employee on the job, or at least being available, in order to help him/her quickly develop the needed basic technical and administrative knowledge.

- Having a checklist of all important functions attached to the job, as stated in the job description.

- Having a training program or plan to help the new employee quickly learn about his/her job.

- Developing a coordination plan with all employees who will be involved in the new employee's tasks and duties.

- Planning a series of visits to customers and/or suppliers to help the new employee get acquainted with the different people involved in the implementation of his/her tasks.

- Having a training and coaching program, including performance appraisals and development action plans.

We suggest that you develop a checklist containing all of these above points, which can show a new employee what you have planned, to ensure a swift, smooth integration into the team and a fast development on the job. And make it part of your employee policy book.

LACK OF APPRECIATION

According to a Gallup survey, 74% of employees are disengaged at work. Disengaged employees will search for an organization that will engage them.[3] Following Leigh Branham (*"The 7 Hidden Reasons Employees Leave"*), the major reasons given for disengagement and departure are: [4]

- **Poor management** - uncaring and unprofessional managers; overworked staff; no respect, no listening, putting people in the wrong jobs; speed valued over quality; poor manager selection processes.

- **Poor communications** - problems communicating top-down and between departments; after mergers; between facilities.

- **Lack of recognition** - that says it all.

- **Poor leadership** - not listening, asking, or investing in employees; unresponsiveness and isolation; mixed messages.

- **Lack of training** - nonexistent or superficial training; nothing for new hires, managers, or to move up.

- **Excessive workload** – being asked to do more with less; also sacrificing quality and customer care to make the numbers.

- **Lack of tools and resources** – inadequate supplies, poor technical support, lack of human resources to relieve overwork.

- **Lack of teamwork** – not enough cooperation and commitment to get the job done; conflicts between departments or services.

When employees feel their contribution is appreciated and valued, that the organization cares about their well-being and is ready to offer help when needed, this is referred to as "perceived organizational support." As reported by *RTWKnowledge.org*, a review of over 70 scientific studies investigated the effects of perceived organizational support, along with the factors that can increase perceived support in the workplace.

The main effects of perceived support are: [5]

1. Increased commitment

2. Improved job satisfaction and mood

3. Increased interest in work

4. Increased performance

5. Decreased psychological strain

6. Increased desire to remain working for the organization

7. Decreased withdrawal (including decreased lateness, absentee-ism and turnover)

Per the same source, there are three main factors that increase perceived organizational support and make employees feel appreciated and cared about. These are: fairness, support and rewards from supervisors and job conditions.

Simply stated, it should be a natural management attitude to appreciate a job well done, to acknowledge employees' intentions to contribute and to recognize their willingness to make things go right.

Yet this is exactly what the majority of employees complain about: their leaders don't care enough!

LACK OF LEADERSHIP

To end off this chapter, we could ask: what is the *first* reason why talented, top players leave a company? The simplest and most condensed answer probably lies in one of the largest studies undertaken by the Gallup Organization. The study surveyed over a million employees and 80,000 managers and was published in a book called "*First Break All The Rules*," by Marcus Buckingham and Curt Coffman.[7]

The findings: if you're losing good people, look to their immediate supervisor. More than anything else, the direct manager is the reason people stay and thrive in an organization. He or she is also the reason why they quit, taking their knowledge, experience and contacts with them — often straight to the competition.

DID YOU KNOW?

**EMPLOYEES STAY FOR REASONS
YOU WOULD NOT SUSPECT**

Beverly Kaye and Sharon Jordan-Evans, authors of the great book *"Love-Em or Lose'Em,"* asked over 17,000 people why they stayed in an organization. They came up with 20 reasons, listed in order of frequency. 91% of respondents listed at least one of the first two items below among the top few reasons they stayed; 98% listed at least one of the first three reasons: [6]

1. Exciting work and challenge
2. Career growth, learning and development
3. Working with great people
4. Fair pay
5. Supportive management/good boss
6. Being recognized, valued and respected
7. Benefits
8. Meaningful work and making a difference
9. Pride in the organization, its mission and its products
10. Great work environment and culture
11. Autonomy, creativity, and sense of control
12. Flexibility, work hours, dress code, etc.
13. Location
14. Job security and stability
15. Diverse, changing work assignments
16. Fun on the job
17. Being part of a team
18. Responsibility
19. Loyalty, commitment to the organization or coworkers
20. Inspiring leadership

"People leave their managers, not their companies," write the authors Marcus Buckingham and Curt Coffman. *"So much money has been thrown at the challenge of keeping good people — in the form of better pay, better perks and better training — when, in the end, turnover is mostly a manager issue."*

If you have a turnover problem, look first to your managers in charge. Are they driving your top players away?

Employees' primary needs seem to have less to do with money and more to do with how they are treated, appreciated and valued. Much of this depends mainly on their supervisor.

A Fortune Magazine survey some years ago found that nearly 75% of employees have suffered at the hands of tough superiors.[8] Of all the workplace stressors, a bad boss is possibly the worst, directly impacting the emotional health and productivity of employees.

So where can the big difference be made? Simply stated, in the way you treat your people. Attitude is the most sought-after soft skill in applicants; it also appears to be a rare quality among employers. The good news is: attitude is free, so you can never show too much of it!

NO-FAIL HIRING TIPS

➲ Over 50% of workers in America quit their job within the first 6 months. The direct costs associated with such a high turnover can amount to hundreds of thousands of dollars. You can avoid most of these costs by applying the law of transparency at the start: make sure that selected applicants fully understand the job description and, most importantly, know about your expectations. Do not hide anything; do not try to portray a better picture than the reality of a job and/or the company. Use any existing challenge to motivate top players and scare others away.

➲ Ensure that the match between the new employee and his/her manager will fit. If a new employee's direct supervisor is a tough person (by nature), make sure that the employee will be able to live with it. Never hire someone without ensuring that he/she will accept the authority of his/her direct manager.

➲ New employees need special attention in many areas, in order to make it through the first months. Use our checklist to plan action on these different areas. Make it part of your employee policy book.

➲ One vital part of attention is on training and getting the new employee at a good level of competency on the job. Create a training/development checklist that will give new employees predictions of their personal enhancement in the company. The best way to show that you care is to help them do a better job by increasing their know-how.

➲ Engaged employees who feel valued and appreciated for their work are more loyal and more motivated. Develop a culture of engagement and of commitment through fairness, support and rewards. This alone will make most of them willing to work hard for you.

➲ If you are losing good people, the first thing to do is to look to your managers and supervisors who are in charge. They may be competent and a good asset to your business – except that if they keep turning good people away, they will keep your business down and non-expanding. Because at the end of the day, your best business asset is people!

When new hires can be productive in their first month, they have a higher morale, a stronger self-confidence and a deeper feeling of involvement. It is your job to help them perform fast!

Chapter

14

Make Them Perform FAST

"Human beings enjoy spending their time engaged in meaningful work. Unfortunately, work is often the last place they turn to, to engage in meaningful work."

Roy M. Spence, Jr.,
Author of *"It's Not What You Sell, It's What You Stand For"* [1]

YOUR MAGIC WEAPON AT WORK _____

The power of a strong job description. In Chapter 4, you read about the importance of formalizing your job description. We did not, however, tell you everything about it. You can use your job description as the ultimate management tool. While most companies either neglect their importance or fail to use them optimally, you should actually consider a job description as your magic weapon.

Why? Simply because a well-developed job description is a self-managing tool that your top players can use starting on their first day of work. Remember, a job description should answer specific questions to help an applicant fully understand what is expected:

1. What is the exact title of the job?

2. In which division, section or unit is this job located?

3. To whom does the employee report?

4. What is the importance of this division in the company activity and what will be its relative importance within the next three to five years?

5. Is this job a new one or is it a vacancy due to a departure?

6. What specific challenges are inherent to this job?

7. What products/services are directly or indirectly handled by the job?

8. What is the target market for these products?

9. What is the purpose of the job – in other words, how does it contribute to the goals and purposes of the company?

10. What are the precise performance/results <u>expectations</u>?

11. How are those result expectations monitored and measured?

12. What are the <u>precise</u> tasks, duties and responsibilities of the job?

13. What are the required technical competencies?

14. What is the desired or required experience?

15. How important is teamwork and coordination of efforts?

16. What are the required personality and behavioral characteristics? Why?

17. What impact could a good or a bad decision on the job have on the division and the company performance?

18. What management style applies to the supervision of the job?

19. What is the planned salary and other compensation?

20. What training program is planned for fast results achievement?

21. What kind of performance appraisal is planned on the job?

22. Does this job offer career development opportunities?

From this job description you can develop a "job performance progress" checklist, showing the important criteria of success on the job as well as any point needing attention. It could look like this:

JOB PERFORMANCE PROGRESS CHECKLIST

NAME: _____ DAY STARTED: _____ JOB: _____

1) **Specific purpose of the job** (how it contributes to the purposes of the company):

_____

_____

_____

2) **Performance/results expectations**

- 1 month: _____

- 3 months: _____

- 6 months: _____

- 1 year: _____

3) **Performance monitoring and measurement**

Statistic No. 1: _____

Statistic No. 2: _____

Statistic No. 3: _____

4) **Precise tasks, duties and responsibilities of the job**

a. _____

b. _____

c. _____

d. _____

e. _____

f. _____

g. _____

h. _____

5. **Most important personality (soft skills) required**

a. _____

b. _____

c. _____

d. _____

e. _____

f. _____

g. _____

h. _____

6. **Planned salary – progress plan**

- Period 1 (3 months): _____

- Period 2 (6 months): _____

- Period 3 (12 months): _____

7. **Planned training program – progress plan**

- Period 1 (3 months): _____

- Period 2 (6 months):_____
- Period3(12months):_____

8. **Planned dates for performance review**

   - 1 month:_____
   - 3months:_____
   - 6months:_____
   - 12months:_____

Progress control. How can you use the original job description and the job performance progress checklist to help a new employee become quickly operational? First, by ensuring that he/she fully understands <u>your expectations</u>. This is precisely what the job description is for.

You are going to have to regularly remind your young recruits of the exact contents of their job descriptions. You are going to have to challenge them on it. You are going to have to make it clear that their whole performance will be monitored against their job description.

The job performance progress checklist is a constant reminder. It allows you to keep control and predict an employee's evolution, from the start. It helps you avoid the 10 most frequent reasons of poor performance on the job (in descending order of importance):

1. **No clear job description**. It always starts here. They don't know what they are supposed to do and why. Fix this by first creating a clear job description. Use the questions and recommendations presented in Chapter 3. You can also find a lot of job description samples on the Internet.

2. **No idea of what the job purpose is.** They must know the reason why they should do what you are asking them to do; otherwise you soon end up with very unmotivated personnel. And the purpose of a job is not to make the boss rich (see later in this chapter, "the group superglue factor").

3. **No idea of expected end results**. Your job description should be, first of all, performance-based. You do not pay them to do things but to achieve something. This is probably the grossest mistake observed in more than 80% of job descriptions: they lead people to develop "busy-ness," rather than real business.

4. **No clear performance monitoring**. Obviously, if you can't measure what you are trying to achieve, you will waste a lot of time and energy trying to achieve it. How do you measure performance for a specific job? If you can't answer that question, do not expect an employee to come up with the answer either!

5. **Lack of know-how**. Too many employers and managers judge their new employees within their first few weeks on the job. If they don't show results fast, they are categorized as low performers. Yet, it is a proven fact that you can multiply an employee's productivity and performance by 20 to 50% in less than a couple of months. How? By helping them improve their competencies. In fact, most new employees will judge their direct manager on that exact point: "How much is my boss willing to share his know-how with me?"

6. **No performance review**. People need direction. They need to know that they are on the right track. Only a very few (less than 10%) will naturally perform by themselves, without your help and your support. A performance review is a great opportunity to communicate openly with an employee about his or her concerns or difficulties.

7. **No recognition for the job done**. We've already covered this topic in Chapter 13. It may seem childish, but your employees need a special type of fuel and that is called appreciation. It does not require daily hugs; it only requires that you make them feel important, because they are. And they will want to do more to the degree that you appreciate what they do.

8. **Personal problems**. An employee may be distracted by some personal, job-unrelated problems. Does this mean that you should get involved? Well, if you want them to perform, you can't ignore the

fact that we all have our personal problems; it sometimes helps to know that someone else will listen! Ignoring your employees' personal problems is like ignoring that your car is running out of gas: you won't go very far with an empty tank.

9. **The employee does not fit with the job.** If that happened too often in the past, you definitely did the right thing when you bought this book. Start implementing it NOW.

10. **The employee would not fit with any job.** Well, that is what happens when you apply blind, emotional hiring. You were really smart when you purchased this book; now you can start with the No-Fail Hiring System and avoid hiring those who could destroy your business faster than fire.

THE BUDDY-SPONSOR FACTOR

Employee orientation challenges. New employees who feel welcomed and are properly taken care of tend to perform better and faster. Additionally, they fit in quickly with colleagues and are readily contributing to new ideas. They speak favorably about your company to friends and relatives. They represent you more confidently with customers, business partners and suppliers.

On the other side, poor orientation of new hires can cost you dearly. According to a study by *Mellon Financial Corp.*, lost productivity resulting from the learning curve for new hires and transfers amounts to between 1% and 2.5% of total revenues. The time for new hires to achieve full productivity ranges from 8 weeks for clerical jobs to 20 weeks for professionals, to more than 26 weeks for executives.[2]

While many employers agree that new employee orientation is critical to good performance and high morale, few actually take the necessary time to ensure that it is done right. As a business owner, you are too busy to "babysit" a new hire, right? After all, you hired them to take over a load off your shoulders, not to add to it!

This is where a *buddy* can help.

A buddy, also called an internal sponsor, is a trusted employee who partners with a new hire during the orientation and job takeover period. He/she is a coordinator, an advisor or even a confidante. He/she is the one the new hire can always go to for any advice, comment or crisis, usually for the first 60 days on the job.

A buddy is NOT the new hire's boss. The purpose of a "buddy system" — as ideally described in a company policy — is to help a new employee from the first day at work to:

- Adapt quickly to the new work environment,
- Start performing fast and
- Feel well taken care of.

The buddy's responsibilities. The buddy is ideally selected with the new employee's personality and character in mind. He/she recognizes that the new employee reports to his/her direct manager and therefore does not try to "manage" his or her protégé. Although you might think that the buddy will become less productive as a consequence of such program, the reverse is usually true. The buddy's role and responsibilities could be:

- Welcoming the new employee at the start and presenting the buddy system with its purpose and rules;
- Making him/her feel welcome and comfortable in his/her new environment;
- Giving tours of the company;
- Introducing other employees and executives;
- Being a source of clarification of policies, procedures, protocols, etc.;
- Taking care of the orientation process;
- Answering all questions, whatever their nature;
- Helping with job description and training procedures;
- Accompanying him/her to staff meetings and to social or company events;

- Being a mediator in case of difficulties or frustrations on the job.

A buddy is really the business owner's or the manager's internal rep with the new employee. You should plan a weekly meeting or lunch with both, during which time you can informally communicate anything. Remember the different reasons why new employees leave, as presented in chapter 13 of this book.

We recommend that your selected buddies read chapter 13. They will be better able to help you ensure that your new top players feel really welcomed and taken care of. By formalizing the buddy-sponsor factor in the company, you allow all your staff to share the responsibility of making new employees happy and productive — fast.

THE MONITORING FACTOR

Employee performance review. A well-conducted performance review is a critical component of employee performance and satisfaction on the job. Employee performance appraisals are usually a "chore" that many business owners and managers dread, mainly because they lack a simple, sound system for conducting those reviews.

Here are a few principles to help you make it easy and even motivativational for both the manager and his/her employee:

1) Establish the correct monitoring criteria. How do you determine performance? What *statistic(s)* should allow the employee – and the manager – to monitor performance? Whatever the job, define one or a few statistics that the employee will be managed on. If you can't measure performance, you can't monitor it in any way.

2) What's the target? The chosen monitoring criteria/statistics have to reflect a target to achieve. Avoid giving long-term targets which do not motivate the employee to work hard right away. Ideally, try to monitor performance on a weekly basis, or at least on a monthly basis. It is easier to control – and easier to correct short-term achievements.

3) Make sure that you set targets and standards, that are realistic to both parties. An employee who does not believe that a target can ever be met, will not always communicate their doubts, but will for sure show resistance and animosity, when you complain about below-target results.

4) Define the purposes of the performance review in an employee policy. Make it clear that the purpose is NOT to punish but to evaluate in order to either improve or correct. Ensure that the employee understands the rules of the game. Invite open communication and comments, suggestions or even concerns.

5) Motivate the employee to formally provide his/her own feedback, prior to the performance review. This will allow you to better understand his/her expectations and concerns, as well as any specific points that needs attention. Invite them to present, in writing, their own viewpoints on current performance, what problems they face and what actions they suggest.

6) Your performance review should always contain the same evaluation points. It is recognized that the following ones are usually the most important ones:
   - Quality of performance
   - Quantity of performance
   - Willingness
   - On-the-job know-how
   - Dependability
   - Team-ability
   - Other behavioral issues
   - Compensation issues

More performance review tips. The first reviews may be stressful for new, and in particular, young employees. Make it easy and safe. It is important to avoid unnecessary anxiety when conducting this important management procedure. The following tips will help:

- <u>Preparation</u>. Have your standard form ready and know beforehand what the main subjects of attention will be. Ensure that the employee has had a chance to present his/her feedback and comments before the meeting.

- <u>Positivity</u>. Focus first on any positive feedback you can give for the recent performance, measured against the eight evaluation points given above. Remind the employee that the purpose of the review is to validate, encourage, improve, correct and/or modify. Avoid unnecessary confrontation or criticism.

- <u>Consistency</u>. Keep the same review evaluation points and criteria at every review session. Compare apples to apples in order to avoid confusion and lack of motivation.

- <u>Listening skills</u>. The review is a good opportunity for the employee to communicate concerns and difficulties, as well as positive feedback. If you do not let them share, they won't. Listening is a great strategy for managing problems and raising natural motivation.

- <u>Communication skills</u>. The review should not be a one-way street. Your job is not to judge but to gather enough information from the employee in order to plan precise action. Ask questions which will allow you to have the correct reality about the employee's viewpoint on his/her performance.

- <u>Compassion</u>. If the employee is facing some work/life imbalance, this is a good time to show compassion and to jointly discuss solutions to improve the balance. You can't, and don't want to avoid this subject, as it is well recognized that private life is often the root of productivity at work.

- <u>Regularity</u>. Stick to the agreed-upon performance review schedule. This contributes to the employee's expectations and stability. It also motivates him/her to keep the pressure on performance.

- <u>Fairness</u>. A non-optimal employee performance is not always caused by a lack of willingness and/or competencies. The company may be partly responsible. It is important to recognize such a fact and to jointly address the points that need improvement, on the management side. Involve the employee in finding solutions. Engaged employees always give back more than you would ask.

- <u>Openness</u>. Stay open to suggestions for procedure improvement or new ideas. Allow the employee to be really involved in the performance appraisal process. They can have good ideas too.

DID YOU KNOW?

**MOST EMPLOYEES HATE
PERFORMANCE REVIEWS**

A 2010 survey reveals what the majority of employees claim are stupid flaws in the annual review process. The survey, conducted by the employee management firm *Taleo*, found: [3]

- 80% of employees are dissatisfied with their company's review process.

- 31% believe there should be a stronger correlation between achieving performance goals and salary.

- 21% feel high-earning employees are treated more fairly in their performance reviews (and rewarded more handsomely) than those with mid- or low-level positions.

- 16% believe performance reviews should occur more than once a year.

THE GROUP SUPERGLUE FACTOR _____

What makes people stick and fight together? What makes them wake up in the morning eager to go to work? Is there one factor which can, by itself, create a natural desire for members of a group to succeed, thrive and spread pride, no matter what the economic conditions are?

Yes, there is. We call it the group superglue factor. It is what many great companies such as Google, Apple, Microsoft, Ikea, BMW, The Container Store, Stonyfield Farms, Trader Joe's, Zappos, Southwest Airlines, etc. have been operating on since day one.

It is Nikos Mourkogiannis' main topic in his book *"Purpose: The Starting Point of Great Companies"* (awarded Business Book of the Year in 2006). Per the author, *purpose* is that single factor that allows leaders to make the best decisions and constantly drive their company ahead of the competition.

Purpose is *the* senior management principle, used to naturally attract and keep highly motivated, creative and loyal employees.

"It does not just mean making money," says Nikos. It is a morale conviction. When a purpose appeals to the moral conviction of employees, then they are more capable of acting with conviction and self-determination, without having to be micromanaged.[4]

Roy Spence, author of the great book *"It's Not What You Sell, It's What You Stand For,"* has extensively studied the effects of being purpose-driven on a business success and on its people's motivation:

"Purpose isn't everything, but it trumps everything else. Sure, every organization must also have strong leadership, management, succession planning, execution, strategy and tactics, innovation and more, but in more than thirty-five years of working with a vast range of companies and organizations, my belief is that it all has to start with a purpose. That is the hinge that everything else hangs upon." [5]

Through his extensive research of purpose-driven companies, Spence has observed that purpose offers up a host of benefits, including easier decision making, deeper employee and customer engagement, and ultimately, more personal fulfillment and happiness. Spence's purpose principles are simple and time-tested: [6]

- **Purpose is the ultimate driver**. It drives all major decisions and is the determining factor in how you allocate resources, hire employees, plan for the future, and judge your success.

- **Purpose leads to high performance**. It fulfills a deep-seated need that people have to thrive for good, valuable reasons; it drives preference for your company.

- **Purpose boosts innovation**. It provides the motivation and direction necessary to create meaningful innovation.

- **Purpose can help you move mountains**. It can rally the troops to overcome seemingly insurmountable odds.

- **Purpose helps you persist in a turbulent marketplace**. It leads you through when times get tough and the road unclear.

- **Purpose energizes your branding strategy**. It is not something you can fake. It's genuine. It's real. And it's something that your customers honestly appreciate about you.

- **Purpose helps you recruit the right people**. It makes your organization more attractive to value-based, passionate people.

- **Purpose boosts energy and vitality**. It provides meaningful and sustainable motivation for employees.

- **Purpose makes people proud**. Work is no longer a routine but a meaningful source of fulfillment and satisfaction.

Tim Sanders, former Chief Solution Officer at Yahoo!, Inc. and author of *"Saving the World at Work,"* puts the value of purpose one step further. He suggests that a *Responsibility Revolution* is now shaking up the corporate world and is leading business owners and leaders to focus on their social responsibilities in order to maintain their competitiveness.

According to Sanders, 65% of American consumers say they would change to brands associated with a good cause if price and quality are equal; 66% of recent college graduates will not work for companies with poor social values. And more than 60 million people are willing to pay a premium for socially and environmentally responsible products. Businesses that do not take this revolution into account are putting their companies at risk.[7]

What does it all mean for you? Simply stated, you can take advantage — at no cost, of the power of a responsible purpose. Whatever the nature of your business is, you can lead the way. Help everyone under your leadership become a positive force for enriching group members, customers, people, communities, and the environment.

When a globally meaningful purpose drives your business, you rally many people around you in a beautiful quest not just for profits, but for what matters most: improvement of conditions for everyone.

More importantly, you attract only people who have a sense of contribution, responsibility and social value. At the end of the day, spending your working hours with top players who share your own values does not require so much managing, but mostly positive guidance and inspiration.

Which do you prefer?

NO-FAIL HIRING TIPS

◒ A well-developed job description is truly your magic weapon – not just to hire but to retain your employees and inspire them to perform fast. It should be the first and a senior employee policy for each new hire to use on a daily basis.

◒ For the employee, the "Job Performance Progress Checklist" is a constant reminder of performance expectations on the job. It allows you to keep control and predict an employee's evolution from the start. It also helps avoid the most frequent reasons of new employees' poor performance within the first 6 months.

◒ The buddy-sponsor factor is a great way to make a new employee's orientation inspiring. It also allows you to use existing employees as mentors for the new arrivals. When well organized, this relationship can be enriching for all. And most importantly, it helps a new hire feel integrated and accepted by the team. Make it a company policy that every employee has to be ready and willing to take a new hire under his/her wings for one to two months.

◒ Employee performance reviews/appraisals are usually dreaded by employees and executives alike. The simple reason is that most managers do not have a structured, well-organized "system." Make performance reviews a vital part of people management and make it a company policy. Use the principles and tips presented in this chapter to structure and standardize your employee performance reviews. For new employees, plan the first formal review as early as after one month. Invite both the employee and his/her buddy-sponsor to attend.

◒ Take advantage of the most powerful management principle, available at no cost: *Purpose*. Get yourself better educated on the subject of "responsibility revolution" and see how you can adapt it to your business activities. We call purpose the "group superglue factor," because it sticks people together around a common cause. Find a way to get your employees to stick around a company purpose that is worth fighting for – no matter what your business is.

Conclusion

"We believe that it's really important to come up with core values that you can commit to. And by commit, we mean that you're willing to hire and fire based on them."

Tony Hsieh,
CEO, Zappos.com, Inc.,
"Delivering Happiness: A Path to Profits, Passion and Purpose" [1]

HIRE HARD AND SMART _____

In the new job market environment, hiring right is going to be your number one challenge. The coming years are going to be tough for any expansion-oriented business. We are facing:

- an unstable economy that will never return to "how it was";

- a more volatile employment market with higher turnovers generating increased operational costs;

- applicants that lack the most vital soft skills needed to develop long-term performance and stability;

- increasing federal and state regulations making it harder for any business owner who aspires to hire for growth; and

- legal risks attached to hiring that are rapidly spreading into the small-to-medium sized companies.

If you are looking to expand your business, you need the competitive edge of a *No-Fail* Hiring System. The smarter you operate, the more you embrace the "new norm," the higher your chances of recruiting the right people who will fight with you, rather than against you – and the less you will have to endure the painful consequences of wrong hires or, God forbid, employment legal cases.

The good news is, NOW is the best time to rally self-motivated, soft-skilled and talented people that have a hard-core necessity to succeed – economically, socially and personally.

With our *No-Fail* Hiring System, you are best armed to recruit those who are willing to work toward a brighter future and to share your passion for performance, profits and purpose. They are out there. Your challenge is not to find them but to ATTRACT them. A better America is in the making; you are the hidden but true source behind it!

To your success in *No-Fail* Hiring,

The authors.

Notes

INTRODUCTION

1) Scott Melland, "The Future of Recruiting," Dice Holdings, Inc. *Marketing.dice*.com 2010. Web. Oct. 25, 2010.

CHAPTER 1:

1) Prosen, Bob. *Kissing Theory Good Bye.* Dallas, TX: Gold Pen Publishing, 2006:31. Print.

2) "Step 1: Why do Businesses Fail and What You Can Learn From These Failures."*Critical Care for Companies.* 2005. Web. Jul. 26, 2010.

3) "Bill Gates Quotes." *ThinkExist.com.* n.d. Web. Jul. 26, 2010.

4) "Lee Iacocca Quotations." *Small BusinessNotes.com.* n.d. Web. Jul. 26, 2010.

5) "Steve Job Quotes." Recruiting & HR Humor. *TalentSpring.com.* n.d. Web. Jul. 26, 2010.

6) "Count Me in for Women's Economic Independence," *CountMeIn.org.*

7) "Hiring Problems." *Eqhelp.com.* Simmons Management Systems. n.d. Web. Jul. 26, 2010.

8) Larocca, Joe. "Five Takeaways From the National Retail Security Survey." *Retail's Big Blog.* National Retail Federation. Oct. 14, 2009. Web. Jul. 26, 2010.

9) Still, Sally and Meghan Lehner. "Curbing Employee Theft." *Human Resource Executive Online.* Sept. 2, 2009. Web. Jul. 26, 2010.

10) Shulman, Terrence. "Biting the Hand That Feeds: the Fastest Growing Crime in America." *EzineArticles.com.* Mar. 12, 2010. Web. Jul. 26, 2010.

11) Maurer, Roy. "OSHA Forms Alliance Focusing on Workplace Violence." *SHRM Online.* Society of Human Resources Management. Mar. 25, 2009. Web. Jul. 26, 2010.

12) Grannis, Kathy. "Troubled Economy Increases Shoplifting Rates, According to National Retail Federation Security Survey." *NRF.com.* National Retail Federation. Jun. 16, 2009. Web. Jul. 26, 2010.

13) "Frequently Asked Questions, No. 2." *SBA.gov.* U.S. Small Business Administration. n.d. Web. Jul. 26, 2010,

CHAPTER 2:

1) Rosen, Lester S. *The Safe Hiring Manual.* Tempe, AZ: Facts on Demand Press, 2007:19. Print.

2) Giuliano, Jim. "What's an employee lawsuit cost these days?" *HRMorning.com.* Jan. 12, 2010. Web. Aug. 8, 2010.

3) "Making the Case for Keeping HR." *HRHero.com.* May 4, 2010. Web. Aug. 8, 2010.

4) Kim Victoria. "Jury awards $2.3 million in LAPD harassment case." *LATimes.com.* Los Angeles Times. Apr. 2, 2009. Web. Aug. 4, 2010.

5) "Judge: BBQ exec must pay sex harassment settlement." *WRAL.com.* Dec. 16, 2008. Web. Aug. 4, 2010.

6) Eligon, John. "Jury Awards Former Tunnel $735,000 in Discrimination Case." *NYTimes.com.* New York Times. Jul. 30, 2008. Web. Aug. 13, 2010.

7) Egan, Mary Ellen. "Novartis Loses Sex Discrimination Case." *Blogs.Forbes.com.* Forbes Magazine. May 18, 2010. Web. Aug. 13, 2010.

8) "Data and Facts on Disputes in the Workplace" *KingMediation.com.* King Mediation Professional Dispute Resolution. n.d. Web. Aug. 13, 2010.

9) See Note (8) above.

10) See Note (8) above.

11) *Tallahassee Furniture Co., Inc. v. Harrison,* 583 So. 2d 744 (Fla. First DCA 1991).

12) Hauswirth, William. "Negligent Hiring: Employer Risk." *Iso.com.* ISO Review. Aug. 2009. Web. Aug. 13, 2010.

13) Pozgar, G. *Legal Aspects of Health Care Administration.* Sudbury, MA: Jones and Bartlett Publishers, Inc., 2004:31. Print.

14) *Quinones v. Roe,* Cal., Los Angeles County Super. Ct., No. BC 076751, Mar. 23, 1994, 37 ATLA L. Rep. No. 10, p. 376 (Dec. 1994)

15) *Butler v. Hertz Corp.,* Pa., Philadelphia County Court of Common Pleas, Apr. Term, 1990, No. 1691, Feb. 11, 1991, reported in 34 ATLA L. Rep. 247 (Sept. 1991).

16) *Porter v. Proffitt's,* Inc., Tenn., Bradley County Cir. Ct., No. V-94-676, Sept. 19, 1996, reported in 40 ATLA L. Rptr. No. 2, p. 72 (March 1997).

17) *Liebman v. Hall Fin. Group, Inc.,* Tex., Dallas County 116th Jud. Dist. Ct., No. 93-07042-F, July 27, 1994, reported in 38 ATLA L. Rep. 149 (May 1995)

18) *McLean v. Kirby Co.,* 490 N.W.2d 229 (N.D. 1992).

19) "Employment Statistics." *American Data Bank.Com* n.d. Web. Aug. 13, 2010.

20) Hansen, Fay. "Avoid Getting Sued: Risks and Rewards in Recruitment Record Keeping." *Workforce.com*. Workforce Management Online. Feb. 2007. Web. Aug. 8, 2010.

21) Taylor, Dave. "How do you fire an employee?" *The Business Blog at Intuitive.com*, Intuitive Systems, n.d. Web. Aug. 13, 2010.

22) "Fact Sheet #21: Recordkeeping Requirements under the Fair Labor Standards Act (FLSA)." *DOL.gov*. U.S. Dept. of Labor, Wage and Hour Division. n.d. Web. Aug. 13, 2010.

23) Muhl, Charles L. "The Employment-At Will Doctrine, Three Major Exceptions," *Monthly Labor Review Online*. Jan. 2001, Vol. 124, No. 1. Web. Aug. 10, 2010.

24) Title VII of the Civil Rights Act of 1964, [42 U.S.C. § 2000e-2(h)]

25) Walsh, David Walsh. *Employment Law for Human Resource Practice*. Mason, OH: South-Western Cengage Learning, 2010:177. Print.

26) "Ford Motor Co., Affiliates, UAW Agree to Pay $1.6 Million to Settle Class Racial Bias Lawsuit." *EEOC.gov*. Equal Employment Opportunity Commission. Dec. 20, 2007. Web. Aug. 10, 2010.

27) "OFCCP Settles Hiring Discrimination Case with The Wackenhut Corp." *AffirmativeActionN.ews.blogspot.com*. Affirmative Action News. Jun. 14, 2010 Web. Aug. 12, 2010.

28) Fact Sheet. "Employment Tests and Selection Procedures." *EEOC.gov*. Equal Employment Opportunity Commission. n.d. Web. Aug. 4, 2010.

29) "Adoption of Questions and Answers To Clarify and Provide a Common Interpretation of the Uniform Guidelines on Employee Selection Procedures, No. 10." *EEOC.gov*. Equal Employment Opportunity Commission. n.d. Web. Aug. 7, 2010. Source: FEDERAL REGISTER, VOL. 44, NO. 43, MARCH 2, 1979.

CHAPTER 3:

1) Collins, Jim Collins. *From Good to Great*. New York, NY: HarperCollins Publishers, Inc., 2001:63. Print.

2) Maltby, Emily. "6 companies born during downturns." *CNNMoney.com*. Cable News Network. n.d. Web. Aug. 10, 2010.

3) Reingold, Jennifer. "Jim Collins: How great companies turn crisis into opportunity." *CNNMoney.com*. Fortune Magazine. Jan. 22, 2009. Web. Aug. 13, 2010.

4) Reich, Robert. "The Future of American Jobs." *HuffingtonPost.com*. April 12, 2009. Web. June 8, 2010.

5) Murray, Sara."Chronic Joblessness Bites Deep." *WSJ.com*. Wall Street Journal. June 2, 2010. Web. Aug. 14, 2010.

6) See Note (5) above.

7) Thomas, Marc. "Unemployment Declines, But the News is Not Good." *MoneyWatch. com*. CBS. Jul. 2, 2010. Web. Aug. 13, 2009.

8) "U6 Unemployment Rate." *Portal Seven.Com*. Society of Human Resource Management. n.d. Web. Aug. 14, 2010.

9) Dougherty, Conor. "Local Governments Still Shedding Jobs." *WSJ.com*. Wall Street Journal. July 2, 2010. Web. Aug. 14, 2010.

10) Bartsch, Kristina J., "Employment Projections 2008 – 2018", *Monthly Labor Review Online*. Nov. 2009, Vol. 132, No. 11. Web. Aug. 14, 2010.

11) Light, Joe. "More Workers Start to Quit." *WSJ.com*. Wall Street Journal. May 25, 2010. Web. Aug. 14, 2010.

12) "Resume Fraud." *Money-Zine.com*. n.d. Web. Aug. 14, 2010.

13) Zupec, Rachel. "Honesty is the Best Policy in Resumes and Interviews." *ReCareerist.com*. n.d. Web. Aug. 14, 2010.

14) "The Problem of Resume Misrepresentations." *Juristaff.com*. Sept. 2008. Web. Aug. 14, 2010. Original source: Repa, Barbara. "Resume Inflation: Two Wrongs May Mean No Rights." Aug. 2001.

15) "Human Resources by the Numbers." *HireRight.com*. n.d. Web. Source: Wall Street Journal, 2003.

16) 2010 Fraud Report to the Nations – Key Findings and Highlights." *ACFE.com*. Association of Certified Fraud Examiners. n.d. Web. Aug. 14, 2010.

17) Schoeff, Mark, Jr., "Companies Report Difficulties in finding Qualified Employees." *Workforce.com*. Workforce Management. Oct. 9, 2009. Web. Aug. 04, 2010.

18) "People and Profitability – a Time for Change." *NAM.org*. Manufacturing Institute. May, 2009. Web. Aug 1, 2010.

19) Klaus, Peggy. *The Hard Truth about Soft Skills*. New York, NY: HarperCollins Publishers, Inc., 2007. Print.

20) Isidore, Chris. "Looking for work? Unemployed need not apply." *CNNMoney.com*. Jun. 16, 2010. Web. Aug. 10, 2010.

21) Cohen, William A. *Secrets of Special Ops Leadership: Dare the Impossible -- Achieve the Extraordinary*. New York, NY: AMACOM, 2006:36. Print.

22) Finegold, David and Susan Morhman. "What Do Employees Really Want – The Perception vs The Reality," *CEO.USC.EDU.* Center for Effective Organizations. World Economic Forum, Jan. 2001. Web. Aug. 1, 2010.

23) Ray, Barry. "Who is afraid of the big bad boss? Plenty of us." *FSU.edu.* Florida State University News. n.d. Web. July 10, 2010.

CHAPTER 4:

1) Kerr, Steve. *Reward Systems: Does Yours Measure Up?* Boston, MA: Harvard Business Press, 2009. Print.

2) Dictionary definition "subjectivity". *Wordreference.com.* Web. Aug. 10, 2010.

3) Moore, Michael."Use of Subjective Hiring Criteria May Require Procedural Safeguards." *PALaborandEmploymentBlog.com.* McNees, Wallace & Nurick, LLC. Jul. 10, 2008. Web. Aug. 10, 2010.

4) "Carter v. Three Springs Residential Treatment."*FindLaw.com* Jan. 06, 1998. Web. Aug. 10, 2010.

5) Clark, Margaret. "Subjectivity Considered Valid in Hiring Decisions." *AllBusiness.com.* HR Magazine. Dec. 1, 2000. Web. Aug. 10, 2010

6) "The Federal Reporter." Vol. 294. 3rd Edit. Jun. 24, 2002. *Resource.* Web. Aug. 10, 2010.

7) See Note (3) above.

8) Fournies, Ferdinand. *Why Don't Employees Do What They're Supposed to Do and What To Do About It,* McGraw-Hill, 2007:3. Print.

9) *USLegalForms.com.* n.d. Web. Aug. 10, 2010.

10) Rosen, Lester S. *The Safe Hiring Manual.* Tempe, AZ: Facts on Demand Press, 2007. Print.

CHAPTER 5:

1) Foster, Michael. *Recruiting on the Web.* McGraw-Hill, 2003:4. Print.

2) Kaneshige, Eugenia . "How long will it take me to find a job?" *NoordwoodAdvisors.com.* Jan.15, 2009. Web. Aug. 20, 2010.

3) Crispin, Gerry. "Meltdown in 2009 and What It Means for a 2010 Recovery." *CareerXroads.com.* Feb. 2010. Web. Aug. 20, 2010.

4) "Small firms offline on Internet recruitment." *YourWebFuture.com.* n.d. Web. Aug. 20, 2010.

5) "Most Businesses Use Social Nets for Hiring." *EMarketer.com.* Jul. 13, 2010. Web. Aug. 20, 2010.

6)   Gildea, Colleen. "Hiring Managers Use Social media in Hiring Process." *Interbiznet.com.* Jun. 12, 2009. Web. Aug. 21, 2010.

7)   Ren, Yuan Li. "Social Media and the Job Hunt." *IBTimes.com.* International Business Times. Jul. 13, 2010. Web. Aug. 21, 2010.

8)   Van Grove, Jennifer. "45% of Employers Now Screen Social Media Profiles." *Mashable. com.* Aug.11, 2009. Web Aug. 21, 2010.

9)   Sullivan, John. "Spend the Summer Rebuilding Your Referral Program and Reap a Bounty of Benefits." *ERE.net.* Jul. 6, 2010. Web. Aug. 20, 2010.

10)   HR World Editors. "Employee Referral Bonus Jackpots: 15 Companies with Awesome New-Hire Incentives." *HRWorld.* Mar. 11, 2008. Web. Aug. 22, 2010.

11)   Gieske, Hans. "Referral Recruiting, Duh!" *ERE.net.* Jul. 14, 2010. Web. Aug. 20, 2010.

CHAPTER 6:

1)   Kleiman, Mel. *Hire Tough – Manage Easy.* Houston, TX: HTG Press, October, 1999:11. Print.

2)   Marquet, Christopher and Lisa Peterson. "Résumé Fraud: The Top 10 Lies." *MarquetIn-ternational.com.* 2005. Web. Aug. 15, 2010.

3)   "Annual Screening Index." *ADP Screening & Selection Services." ADP.com.* Dec. 8, 2009. Web. Aug. 20,2010.

4)   Zupek, Rachel. "Infamous Résumé Lies." MSN.*Careerbuilder.com.* n.d. Web. Aug. 15, 2010.

5)   Tuna, Cari. & Keith J. Winstein."Economy Promises to Fuel Résumé Fraud." *WSJ.com.* Wall Street Journal. Nov. 17, 2008. Web. Aug. 15, 2010.

6)   See Note (2) above.

7)   "Résumé Fraud." *Money-zine.com.* n.d. Web. Aug. 15, 2010.

8)   Tuna, Cari. & Keith J. Winstein. "Economy Promises to Fuel Résumé Fraud." *WSJ.com.* Wall Street Journal. Nov. 17, 2008. Web. Aug. 15, 2010.

9)   Morrison, Mark. "RadioShack's Lesson: Trust, but Verify." *BusinessWeek.com.* Feb. 22, 2006. Web. Aug. 15, 2010.

10)   Revkin, Andrew. "Young Bush appointee resigns his post at NASA." *NYTimes.com.* Feb. 8, 2006. Web. Aug. 10, 2010.

11)   TSC Staff. "Veritas CFO Resigns over Falsified Resume."*TheStreet.Com.* Oct. 3, 2002. Web. Aug.10, 2010.

CHAPTER 7:

1) Carbonara, Peter. "Hire for Attitude, Train for Skills", *FastCompany.com*. Fast Company Magazine, Issue 4. Aug. 31, 1996. Issue 4. Web. Aug. 15, 2010.

2) Senior, Carl & Michael Butler. "Interviewing Strategies in the Face of Beauty: A Psychophysiological Investigation into the Job Negotiation Process." *Annals of the New York Academy of Sciences.* Nov. 2007: Vol. 1118. See also "Who Knew? Good Looking People Get Better Jobs." *EurekAlert.org.* Advancing Science Serving Society. Dec. 6, 2007. Web. Aug. 15, 2010.

3) Kleiman, Mel. *Hire Tough, Manage Easy.* Houston, TX: HTG Press, 1999:31. Print.

4) Lowe, Scott. "Hiring New People – Choosing Between Skills and Attitude." *TechRepublic.com.* Jun. 30, 2009. Web. 15 Aug. 2010.

5) Green, Paul. *Building Robust Competencies: Linking Human Resource Systems to Organizational Strategies.* San Francisco, CA: Jossey-Bass, Inc. Publishers, 1999. Print.

6) Kessler, Robin. *Competency-Based Interviews: Master the Tough New Interview Style And Give Them the Answers That Will Win You the Job.* Franklin Lakes, NJ: The Career Press, Inc., 2006. Print.

7) Loten, Angus. "Younger Employees Lack Basic Skills", *Inc.com.* Oct. 27, 2006. Web. Aug. 15, 2010.

8) Definition of personality – persona, Webster's Encyclopedic Unabridged Dictionary.

9) Murphy,Mark."Why New Hires Fail." *LeadershipIQ.com.* n.d. Web. Aug. 15, 2010.

10) Lancaster, Lynne C. and David Stillman. *The M-Factor: How the Millennial Generation Is Rocking the Workplace.* New York, NY: HarperCollins Publishers, 2010:50-51. Print.

CHAPTER 8:

1) Seinfeld, Jerry. *Sein Language.* Bantam Books. September, 1993:9. Print.

2) *Modtland v. Mills Fleet Farm, Inc.* FPKC. Nov. 28, 2004. Web. 10 Aug. 10, 2010.

CHAPTER 9:

1) Betsy Morris, Interview with Steve Jobs on his Management Style. *Money.CNN.com* Fortune Magazine. Mar. 7, 2008. Web. Aug. 15, 2010.

2) Cornell University Law School. 42 U.S.C. § 12112 (d)(2) A . Law.Cornell.Edu. Cornell University Law School. n.d. Web. Aug. 15, 2010.

3) Cornell University Law School. 42 U.S.C. § 12112(d)(3). Law.Cornell.Edu. Cornell University Law School. n.d. Web. Aug. 15, 2010.

4) Cornell University Law School. 42 U.S.C. § 12112(d)(3)(A). Law.Cornell.Edu. Cornell University Law School. n.d. Web. Aug. 15, 2010.

5) Cornell University Law School. 42 U.S.C. § 12112(d)(3)(B). Law.Cornell.Edu. Cornell University Law School. n.d. Web. Aug. 15, 2010.

6) Cornell University Law School. 42 U.S.C. § 12112(d)(3)(C)-(4)(A). *Law.Cornell.Edu.* Cornell University Law School. Web. Aug. 15, 2010.

7) Wolfe, Ira. "10 Reasons Hiring Managers Fear Pre-Employment Tests." *EzineArticles.* n.d. Web. Aug. 15, 2010.

8) Wolfe, Ira. *The Perfect Labor Storm 2.0.* Bloomington, IN: Xlibris, Corp., Aug. 25, 2007. Print.

9) Mike Poskey, "Myths of Psychological Testing For Candidate Selection," *hodu.com.* n.d. Web. Oct. 30, 2010.

CHAPTER 10:

1) Hoffman, Auren. "The Power of Great People." *Blog.Summation.net.* Feb.1, 2008. Web. Aug. 15, 2010.

2) Griffith, Richard. L. *A Closer Examination of Application Faking Behavior.* Charlotte, NC: Information Age Publishing, Inc., 2006:6-7. Print.

3) Miler, Stephen."Salary Survey Projects Modest U.S. Increases for 2011." *SHRM.org.* Society for Human Resource Management. Jul. 14, 2010. Web. Aug. 15, 2010.

4) Hollon, John."Salary Increase for 2011: What Part of 3% don't you Understand?" *TLNT. com.* Jul.1, 2010. Web. Aug. 15, 2010.

CHAPTER 11:

1) Fishman, Nick. "Trends in Employment Background Screening: 2010 Results" The Verifier. Aug. 2010, Issue XXI:13. *EmployeeScreen.com.* Web. Sep. 1, 2010.

2) See Note (1) above.

3) "Negligent Hiring and Retention: Are You Prepared?" *ReferenceCheck.com/Whats_New.* n.d. Web. Oct. 5, 2010.

4) See Note (3) above.

5) Bachman, Ronet. "Violence and Theft in the Workplace," National Crime Victimization Survey. *bjs.ojp.usdoj.gov.* Bureau of Justice Statistics, U.S. Department of Justice. July, 1994. Web. Oct. 5, 2010. See pages 1-2.

6) "Why Conduct Background Checks?" *Consumer Credentials.com.* n.d. Web. Oct. 5, 2010.

7) Neuman, J.H., and R. A. Baron. "Aggression in the Workplace," in R. A. Giacalone & Jerald Greenberg (Editors). *Antisocial Behavior in Organizations.* Greenwich, CT: Sage Publications, Inc., 1997:37-67. Print.

8) Anderson, L.B., and Smith, Janice E. (June, 1998). "Going Postal: Fact or Fiction?" Presentation at the Society for Human Resource Management National Conference, Minneapolis, MN, June, 1998. Quoted by Hua Wang, "Negligent Hiring: The Emerging Contributor to Workplace Violence in the Public Sector." *AllBusiness.com* Jun. 22, 2001. Web. Oct. 5, 2010.

9) See Note (5) above.

10) "The Ultimate Guide to Conducting Background Checks." *IntegraScan.com.* n.d. Web. Oct. 5, 2010.

11) Aldrich, Catherine. "The Devil Inside: The Legal Liabilities of Background Screening." *AllBusiness.com.* Risk Management Magazine. Feb. 1, 2007. Web. Oct. 5, 2010.

12) See Note (11) above.

13) workplaceviolence911.com/docs/fl.htm, n.d. Web, February 5, 2011.

CHAPTER 12:

1) Welch, Jack. *Winning.* New York, NY: HarperCollins Publishers, 2005:81. Print.

2) "Over Half of Unemployed Workers With Job Offers Said the Pay Was More Than 25% Below Previous Salary, New Personified Survey Finds." *PRNewswire.com.* CareerBuilder Press Release. Sept. 23, 2010. Web. Oct. 25, 2010.

CHAPTER 13:

1) Branham, Leigh. *The 7 Hidden Reasons Employees Leave: How To Recognize The Subtle Signs and Act Before It's Too Late.* Danvers, MA: AMACOM, 2005:36. Print.

2) See Note (1), page 33.

3) Kelley, Tim. "Why Your Employees Don't Care Whether Your Company Succeeds." *TranscendentSolutions.com.* Sept. 8, 2005. Web. Oct. 10, 2010.

4) See Note (1), pages 22-24.

5) Rhoades, L. and R. Eisenberger. "Perceived Organizational Support: A Review of the Literature." Journal of Applied Psychology, 2002, Vol. 87(4):698-714. Summarized in "What is the effect of an employer being supportive, valuing and caring for their employees?" *RTWKnowledge.org.* n.d. Web. Oct. 10, 2010.

6)   Kaye, Beverly & Sharon Jordan-Evans. *Love' Em or Lose' Em: Getting Good People to Stay.* San Francisco, CA: Berret-Koehler Publishers, Inc., 2008:13. Print.

7)   Buckingham, Marcus and Curt Coffman. *First Break All The Rules: What the World's Greatest Managers Do Differently.* New York, NY: Simon & Schuster, 1999. Print.

8)   Kiechel, Walter. "Dealing with the Problem Boss." *CNNMoney.com.* Fortune Magazine. Aug. 12, 1991. Web. Oct. 14, 2010.

CHAPTER 14:

1)   Spence, Roy M., Jr. & Rushing, Haley, *It's Not What You Sell, It's What You Stand For: Why Every Extraordinary Business is Driven by Purpose.* New York, NY: The Penguin Group, 2009:25. Print.

2)   Rollag, Keith, Salvatore Parise and Robb Cross. "Getting New Hires up to Speed Quickly." MIT Sloan Management Review. Winter 2005, Vol. 46, No. 2, *sloanreview.mit.edu.* Web. Oct. 15, 2010.

3)   Hill, Bob. "Why 80% of Employees Hate Annual Reviews." *BusinessBrief.com.* Apr. 12, 2010. Web. Oct. 15, 2010.

4)   Nikos Mourkogiannis, "The Search for Purpose." *NikosOnline.com.* Jun. 21, 2008. Web. Oct. 14, 2010.

5)   See Note (1) above, page 10.

6)   See Note (1) above, page 33.

7)   Sanders, Tim. *Saving the World at Work.* New York: DoubleDay, 2008. Print.

CONCLUSION:

1)   Hsieh, Tony. *Delivering Happiness: A Path to Profits, Passion, and Purpose.* New York, N.Y.: Hachette Book Group, Inc., 2010:154. Print.

Web Resources

NO-FAIL HIRING RESOURCES

For clients who have attended our No-Fail Hiring workshop, the following documents can be accessed at our website for free download. Simply visit www.nofailhiring.com and log in to download your selected document(s) or template(s):

- Checklist of questions for developing a job description
- Samples of company hiring policy
- Sample hiring guidelines
- Tips on writing a recruitment advertisements
- Job advertisement checklist
- Soft skills justification form
- Checklist for resume screening
- Sample job application form
- Checklist for job application screening
- Sample soft skills table
- Checklist of questions to ask when checking references

OTHER RESOURCES

- **Small Business Administration** at www.sba.gov: The U.S. Small Business Administration (SBA) was created in 1953 as an independent agency of the Federal Government to aid, counsel, assist and protect the interests of small business concerns, to preserve free competitive enterprise and to maintain and strengthen the overall economy of our nation. The SBA helps Americans start, build and grow businesses and provides information on business regulations.

- **Equal Employment Opportunity Commission (EEOC)** at www. eeoc.gov: the EEOC is responsible for enforcing federal laws that make it illegal to discriminate against a job applicant or an employee because of the person's race, color, religion, sex (including pregnancy), national origin, age (40 or older), disability or genetic information. Most employers with at least 15 employees are covered by EEOC laws (20 employees in age discrimination cases). Most labor unions and employment agencies are also covered. The laws apply to all types of work situations, including hiring, firing, promotions, harassment, training, wages, and benefits.

- **Bureau of Labor Statistics (BLS)** at www.bls.gov: The BLS is the principal fact-finding agency for the Federal Government in the broad field of labor economics and statistics. The BLS is an independent national statistical agency that collects, processes, analyzes, and disseminates essential statistical data to the American public, the U.S. Congress, other federal agencies, state and local governments, business, and labor. You can access a multitude of data on the economy, employment, productivity, wages, etc.

- **Society for Human Resource Management (SHRM)** at www.shrm.org: SHRM is a global membership organization with more than 250,000 members. They have members in 140 countries and offices in India and China. It provides a community for human resource professionals, media, governments, non-governmental organizations, businesses and academic institutions to share expertise and create innovative solutions on people management issues. It also proposes very informative newsletters, articles, books and essays on the subject of hiring and retention.

- **The Association of Certified Fraud Examiners (ACFE)** at www.acfe.com: The ACFE is the world's largest anti-fraud organization and premier provider of anti-fraud training and education. Together with nearly 55,000 members, the ACFE is reducing business fraud worldwide and inspiring public confidence in the integrity and objectivity within the profession. It provides training and certifications as well as a vast array of information and books on the subject of fraud and crime prevention.

- **The National Association of Colleges and Employers (NACE)** at www.nace.org: The NACE is the leading source of information on the employment of the college educated. The professional association connects more than 5,200 college career services professionals at nearly 2,000 colleges and universities nationwide, and more than 3,000 HR/staffing professionals focused on college relations and recruiting. NACE forecasts trends in the job market; tracks legal issues in employment, the job search, and hiring practices; and provides college and employer professionals with benchmarks for their work.

- **U.S. Legal Forms, Inc**. at www.uslegalforms.com: U.S. Legal Forms, Inc. is the leading publisher of state specific legal forms over the Internet. The company provides legal documents for attorneys, small businesses and consumers. U.S. Legal Forms, Inc., was founded by attorneys and employs a staff of attorneys and professionals that maintain the site and the products provided online.

- **Online social network referral services**: These companies offer support services specializing in social media recruitment and referral hires. Visit jobvite.com, jobster.com, selectminds.com, etc.

- **Online job sites/online job searches**: These web-based companies offer job postings and job search data, allowing employers to post their job vacancies and applicants to post their resumes. There are literally thousands of sites proposing such services. The following are

General

4Jobs.com	CareerJournal.com
50StateJobs.com	ChiliJobs.com
AllJobsFilled.com	Emacjobs.com
American Preferred	EmployerIndex.com
AmericasJobSource	GigFish
Bakos Group	HireAbility.com
Best Jobs USA	HireBreed
Beyond.com	Hireforjobs
Career Exposure	HireNet
CareerBuilder.com	HotResumes.com

Job Bank USA

Job.com

JobAnimal.com

JobCentral.com

JobGuru.com

JobNugget.com

JobPostingsOnline

JobSearchSite.com

JobsExcite

JobsRadar

Jobvertise

Joined

Kakoon.com

MegaJobSites.com

Monster.com

NationalJobBank

Net-Temps

PostResume.com

QuintCareers.com

SearchEase.com

SmartHunt

TalentSpider

The Talent Bank

Thingamajob.com

USJobNetwork.com

Yahoo! HotJobs

ZillionResumes

Technology

devBISTRO

Dice

IS All Stars

ITclassifieds

ITworld.com

JavaJobs

LookTech.com

ProgrammingCareers

TechCareers.com

TechEmployment

Accounting

AccountantCareers

AccountingBoard.com

AccountingClassifieds

AccountingProfessional

Bankingboard.com

Bankjobs.com

FinancialPositions

Sales and Marketing

AccountManager

AdAgeTALENTWorks

HotSalesJobs.com

MediaJobMarket

SalesCareerForum.com

Sales Classifieds

SalesGravy

SalesHeads

SalesJobs.com

the most popular:

- Uniform Guidelines on Employee Selection Procedures at www.gpo. gov: These guidelines incorporate a single set of principles which are designed to assist employers, labor organizations, employment agencies, and licensing and certification boards to comply with requirements of federal law prohibiting employment practices which discriminate on grounds of race, color, religion, sex, and national origin. They are designed to provide a framework for determining the proper use of tests and other selection procedures. These guidelines do not require a user to conduct validity studies of selection procedures where no adverse impact results. However, all users are encouraged to use selection procedures which are valid, especially users operating under merit principles.

- United States Average Salaries at www.worldsalaries.org/usa.shtml: This site provides average salary data per job category. The International Average Salary Income Database provides an international comparison of average salary for various professions and an international comparison of average personal income and expenditures. The data is gathered from publications and reports obtained from government agencies.

- More information on average salaries per job category can also be found at the Bureau of Labor Statistics at www.bls.gov.

- Finding Background Check Firms at www.employmentverification-guide.com: This site provides a nationwide list of background check companies. It is a fast and easy guide to finding a background screener to use when you are conducting investigative checks on potential employees. It allows the user to browse through their national alphabetical list of screening companies. You can also narrow your search by states.

- **Other resources:** Following are some of the websites the authors used to collect data and statistics related to the subject of hiring. They appear below in the sequence that they were used to construct the book, chapter by chapter:

- marketing.dice.com
- thinkexist.com
- smallbusinessnotes.com
- talentspring.com
- eqhelp.com
- ezinearticles.com
- shrm.com
- sba.gov.
- hrmorning.com
- insidecounsel.com
- forbes.com
- mediate.com
- iso.com
- americandatabank.com
- nrf.com
- businessknowhow.com
- dol.gov
- eeoc.gov
- money.cnn.com
- huffingtonpost.com
- online.wsj.com
- pewtrusts.org
- moneywatch.bnet.com
- portalseven.com
- money-zine.com
- careebuilder.com
- hireright.com

- acfe.com
- bettersoftskills.com
- wordreference.com
- findlaw.com
- allbusiness.com
- uslegalforms.com
- careerxroads.com
- yourwebfuture.com
- jobvite.com
- interbiznet.com
- ibtimes.com
- mashable.com
- ere.net
- hrworld.com
- marketinternational.com
- adp.com
- money-zine.com
- nytimes.com
- thestreet.com
- fastcompany.com
- eurekalert.org
- techrepublic.com
- inc.com
- leadershipiq.com
- fpkc.com
- lawcornell.edu
- perfectlaborstorm.com

- tlnt.com
- employeescreen.com
- referencechecks.com
- consumercredentials.com
- intergrascan.com
- accuratebackground.com
- employmentverification-guide.com

- transcendentsolutions.com
- rtwknowledge.org
- chrmglobal.com
- itsnotwhatyousell.com
- businessbrief.com
- nikosonline.com
- savingtheworld.net

Suggested Readings

- *Kiss Theory Good Bye* – Bob Prosen.

- *The Safe Hiring Manual*– Lester S. Rosen, Esq.

- *The Safe Hiring Audit* – *The Employer's Guide to Implementing a Safe Hiring Program* – Lester S. Rosen, Esq.

- *From Good to Great* – Jim Collins.

- *How The Mighty Fall – And Why Some Companies Never Give In* – Jim Collins.

- *The Hard Truth about Soft Skills* – Peggy Klaus.

- *Reward Systems – Does Yours Measure Up?* – Steve Kerr

- *Why Don't Employees Do What They're Supposed to Do and What To Do About It* – Ferdinand Fournies.

- *Recruiting on the Web* – Michael Foster.

- *Hiring the Best – A Manager's Guide to Effective Interviewing and Recruiting* – Martin Yate, C.P.C.

- *Hire Tough – Manage Easy* – Mel Kleiman.

- *Building Robust Competencies* – Paul Green.

- *Competency-based Interviews: Master the New Interview Style and Give Them the Answers That Will Win You the Job* - Robin Kessler.

- *The M-Factor, How the Millennial Generation is Rocking the Workplace* – Lynne C. Lancaster and David Stillman.

- *Winning* – Jack Welch.

- *The 7 Hidden Reasons Employees Leave: How To Recognize The Subtle Signs and Act Before It's Too Late* – Leigh Branham.

- *Love' Em or Lose' Em – Getting Good People to Stay* – Beverly Kaye and Sharon Jordan-Evans.

- *First Break All The Rules – What the World's Greatest Managers Do Differently* – Marcus Buckingham and Curt Coffman.

- *Purpose - The Starting Point of Great Companies* – Nikos Mourkogiannis.

- *It's Not What You Sell, It's What You Stand For – Why Every Extraordinary Business is Driven by Purpose* - Roy M. Spence, Jr. & Haley Rushing.

- *Saving the World at Work* – Tim Sanders.

- *Delivering Happiness – A Path to Profits, Passion and Purpose* – Tony Hsieh.

- *Megatrends 2010 – The Rise of Conscious Capitalism* – Patricia Aburdene.

- *How to Hire A Players – Finding the Top People for Your Team – Even if You Don't Have a Recruiting Department* – Eric Herrenkohl.

- *Get Rid of the Performance Review* – Samuel A. Culbert & Lawrence Rout.

- *WHO – Solve your # 1 Problem* – Geoff Smart & Randy Street.

Index

Glossary

Arson: Criminal act of deliberately setting fire to property

Benchmarking: The process of comparing one's business processes and performance metrics to industry bests and/or best practices from other industries..

Bribery: Act of persuading someone to act in one's favor, typically illegally or dishonestly, by a gift or money or other inducement.

Contingency: A future event or circumstance that is possible but cannot be predicted with certainty.

Damocles' sword: A legendary courtier who extravagantly praised the happiness of Dionysius I, ruler of Syracuse. To show him how precarious this happiness was, Dionysius seated him at a banquet with a sword hung by a single hair over his head. Meaning the ever existent peril.

Embezzlement: to steal or misappropriate money placed in one's trust.

Employment model: Something considered as a standard of excellence to be imitated.

Entrepreneur: Risk taking business person.

Fair Credit Reporting Act: A United States federal law that regulates the collection, dissemination, and use of consumer information, including consumer credit information.

Formalize: To give something a definite form; to shape; make official or legitimate by the observance of proper procedure.

Functional Resumes: Resumes that highlight an applicant's specific experience and skills rather than a chronological listing of work history experience. Functional resumes are often used to emphasize specific experience or to de-emphasize limited experience.

IRS, DOL, EEOC: Internal Revenue Service, Department of Labor, Employee Equal Opportunity Commission

Law of Transparency: As used in the humanities and in a social context more generally, implies openness, communication, and accountability. It is a metaphorical extension of the meaning a "transparent" object is one that can be seen through. Transparent procedures include open meetings, financial disclosure statements, freedom of information legislation, budgetary review, audits, etc.

Leverage: Dealing with the power to get things done and the power over circumstances that gives advantage over others to accomplish something

Manna: (From the Bible) The substance miraculously supplied as food to the Israelites in the Wilderness. (Exodus 16)

Maverick: An independent thinker who refuses to conform to the accepted views on a subject.

Micromanagement: To manage, direct, or control a person, group, or system to an unnecessary level of detail or precision.

Millenial Generation: The generation born 1977-1998.

Optimal: Most desirable or Favorable.

Pilferage: Act of stealing things of relatively little value.

Proclivity: Tendency to choose or do something regularly.

Referral Services: An online referral service is an e-mail job distribution method paid for by employers.

Russian Roulette: A stunt in which you spin the cylinder of a revolver that is loaded with only one bullet and then point the muzzle at your head and pull the trigger.

Social Networking: Social networking is linking people to each other in some way. Social networking sites bring people together who people interested in a particular subject.

Soft skills: A sociological term relating to a person's "EQ" (Emotional Intelligence Quotient), the cluster of personality traits, social graces, communication, language, personal habits, friendliness, and optimism that characterize relationships with other people...

Standardization: to remove variations and irregularities in something and make all types or examples of it the same or bring them into conformity with one another.

Taint: To contaminate or pollute.

Tom Tom Drums Law: The tom-tom drum itself comes from Asian or Native American cultures. The tom-tom drum is also a traditional means of communication. The law here refers to hear it once and then apply it using your own resourcefulness and ability.

To buy more copies of this book or for more information on our hiring training/coaching services and any other services, contact our customer service department at M2-TEC USA, Inc. at 877-831 2299.

You can also send a fax to (727) 449 0979 or e-mail at info@m2-tec.com.

Websites:
www.nofailhiring.com
www.m2-tec.com